Direct Bible Discovery

DIRECT BIBLE DISCOVERY

Ronald W. Leigh

BROADMAN PRESS
Nashville, Tennessee

4211-39

ISBN: 0-8054-1139-9

Unless otherwise marked, Scripture quotations are from *The New American Standard Bible.* Copyright © The Lockman Foundation, 1960, 1962, 1963, 1971, 1972, 1973, 1975. Used by permission.

Dewey Decimal Classification: 220.7

Subject heading: BIBLE—STUDY

Library of Congress Catalog Number: 81-67203

Printed in the United States of America

Appreciation is expressed to Stanley and Dorothy Leigh, to Clark Reynolds, and to many students for their suggestions. My special thanks go to Dr. Mary LeBar for guidance through my first extended experience in inductive Bible study, and to my wife, Karen, for her contributions in every aspect of this work.

"No student of the Scriptures should be satisfied to traffic only in the results of the study of other men. The field is inexhaustible and its treasures ever new. No worthy astronomer limits his attention to the findings of other men, but is himself ever gazing into the heavens both to verify and to discover; and no worthy theologian will be satisfied alone with the results of the research of other theologians, but will himself be ever searching the Scriptures. However, a full-rounded introduction is needed and a method of study must be established if either the astronomer or the theologian expects to continue with ever increasing efficiency."

Lewis Sperry Chafer
Systematic Theology
(Dallas: Dallas Seminary
Press, 1947), p. vi.

Contents

1. Introduction 13
2. How the Holy Spirit Helps 19
3. The Importance of Procedure 27
4. The Direct Procedure 37
5. The Discovery Procedure 45
6. The Order of the Elements 55
7. Observation 59
8. Sample Observations 67
9. Pitfalls and Perseverance in Observation 75
10. Interpretation 83
11. Literary Interpretation 97
12. Contextual Interpretation 107
13. Proper Reasoning 121
14. Application 131
15. Where to Start 137
16. Other Practical Matters 147
17. The Procedure for Studying Books 159
    Procedures Versus Meaning 159
    The Procedure 161
    Step 1—Pray 162
    Step 2—Survey 162
    Step 3—Divide 165
    Step 4—Scrutinize 167
    Step 5—Examine Topics 181
    Step 6—Synthesize 181

Step 7—Compare 182
Step 8—Apply............................. 182
18. The Procedure for Studying Topics 185
Step 1—Pray 185
Step 2—Delimit 186
Step 3—Recall 186
Step 4—Find and Sort 186
Step 5—Scrutinize 190
Step 6—Synthesize 195
Step 7—Compare 195
Step 8—Apply........................... 195
19. Summary: Thirty Key Principles of Bible Study .. 197
Appendix A: Sample Results from a Book Study 201
Appendix B: Sample Results from a Topic Study..... 211
Appendix C: Sample Respaced Texts 231
Appendix D: Diagrams and Examples of
   Types of Relationships 235
Appendix E: A Note to Pastors and Teachers 245
Annotated Bibliography 247
Index 251

Table of Selected Charts, Diagrams, and Lists

The indirect (dependent) approach 37

The direct (independent) approach 39

Bible study aids, noninterpretive
    and interpretive 43

Induction 46

Deduction 47

The extending-assumptions (deductive) approach . . . 49

The discovery (inductive) approach 50

The order of the elements 56

Observation/Interpretation 60

Figures of speech 99

Application in our situation 133

Bible books by categories 140

Model of a Bible book chart 168

Observation-interpretation-application form 170

Types of relationships 178

Servant, diakonos, and related words 188

1

Introduction

If you are a Christian, you already recognize that the Bible is very, very important to us. Our salvation stems from its message of good news. Our values and beliefs are based on its teachings. And our daily lives are guided by its many practical principles. In other words, *our entire Christian experience is based on the Bible, the Word of God. Yet, most Christians have very little direct input from the Bible!* Many Christians' beliefs come primarily from their parents and their pastor rather than from their own *direct* study of the Bible. In view of the great importance of the Bible, all capable Christians should engage in regular, meaningful, direct Bible study. However, except for occasional Bible reading, many Christians think of the Bible as a closed book, to be opened only by the specialists. It is almost as if the Protestant Reformation had never taken place!

One of the central thrusts of the Reformation was that the Bible should no longer be the exclusive property of the church authorities. The Reformers believed that every individual should be able to read the Bible in his own language and should be free to interpret and respond to the Bible on his own, without having to depend on the church officials. That is why Luther gave the Germans the Bible in their own language. Has the Reformation caught up with you? Do you have confidence in your own ability to study the Bible? Or are you depending mostly on *your* church authorities (your pastor, Sunday School teacher, or seminary or Bible college professor) to tell you what the Bible says and means?

What would you think of a person who is handed a telegram but does not look at it, or reads only the first sentence? What would you think of a person who hears someone describe a sunset but does not turn his head to look? Are we any different when we have a message from God and ignore it, or remain satisfied with a mere occasional reading of it, or merely let others tell us what it says?

Your own personal study of the Bible *can* be meaningful and rewarding, but you must know *how* to go about it. This guidebook explains the principles and the step-by-step procedures which will help you discover the correct interpretation of the Bible on your own. This approach to personal Bible study is called *Direct Bible Discovery.* (The initials "DBD" are used throughout this guidebook to stand for *Direct Bible Discovery.*)

A Definition

DBD is an *independent, inductive* approach to personal Bible study. It is a method of studying the Bible in which you go *directly* to the biblical text and examine it for yourself without becoming dependent on interpretive helps. Your main task is to *discover* what the text actually teaches, rather than to assume certain teachings and then go to the text in order to confirm those teachings.

DBD could easily be called Analytic Bible Meditation. This type of meditation is not to be confused with Transcendental Meditation. Bible meditation should be active, verbal, analytic, and reasoning. In contrast, Transcendental Meditation and other Eastern forms of meditation are much more mystical, since they are basically passive, nonverbal, distinctionless, and intuitive. But there is nothing mystical about proper Bible meditation.

Bible meditation has become a lost art, in spite of the fact that meditation and its benefits are repeatedly mentioned in the Bible itself.

> I will meditate on Thy precepts. (Ps. 119:15)

> Let your mind dwell on these things. (Phil. 4:8)

> This book of the law shall not depart from your mouth, but you shall meditate on it day and night, so that you may be careful to do according to all that is written in it; for then you will make your way prosperous, and then you will have success. (Josh. 1:8)

> His delight is in the law of the Lord,
> And in His law he meditates day and night.
> And he will be like a tree firmly planted by streams of water,
> Which yields its fruit in its season,
> And its leaf does not wither;
> And in whatever he does, he prospers.
> (Ps. 1:2-3)

> O how I love Thy law!
> It is my meditation all the day.
> Thy commandments make me wiser than my enemies,
> For they are ever mine.
> I have more insight than all my teachers,
> For Thy testimonies are my meditation.

I understand more than the aged,
Because I have observed Thy precepts
(Ps. 119:97-100)

The use of DBD can recover this meditation for you.

What This Guidebook Is and Is Not

This guidebook *is* an explanation of the principles and procedures which an individual should use in his personal Bible study.

This guidebook is *not* a study guide for use in studying a particular book or topic of the Bible. Study guides (such as *A Study Guide on the Book of Romans* or *A Study Guide on Prayer*) which list a series of questions for studying one particular book or topic are, of course, limited to that book or topic. This guidebook explains the principles and procedures which can and should be applied to the study of *every* book and topic in the Bible.

This guidebook is *not* a discussion of a dozen or more "methods" of Bible study, as some books claim to be. (Actually, such books do not discuss different and distinct *methods* of studying the Bible.) It is best to think in terms of just *one basic approach* which suits all books and topics in the Bible, and then make minor adjustments and additions to the study procedure for special kinds of topics and special kinds of literature.

This guidebook is *not* a presentation of the results of Bible study, as are many books bearing titles such as *Bible Study Methods*. It is not the intent of this guidebook to supply you with an outline of each book of the Bible or with the conclusions of any topical studies. Rather, this guidebook is designed to help you become less dependent on such aids and to arrive at your own results in Bible study.

Chapters 17 and 18 contain the actual steps for Bible study, and these two chapters are laid out like a procedure manual for a definite reason. Many people never get started in proper Bible study procedure because they lack specific, practical, step-by-step guidance. Chapters 17 and 18 are intended to answer the questions, "What exactly do I do first? What exactly do I do next?" etc. However, *do not jump ahead* to chapters 17 and 18. The procedures given in those chapters will make much better sense to you after you have read the first sixteen chapters. Read this entire guidebook straight through and then put chapters 17 and 18 to use. (Suggestions regarding books and topics with which to begin your study are given later.)

DBD can be used by a wide range of people: college students, people without college educations, laymen, pastors—anyone who seriously wants to understand the Bible firsthand. If you have a Bible and can read, you can begin. You do not need any special abilities or a lot of expensive reference books to start.

Our Attitude and Motivation

As in many other areas of life, two of the most important factors which will determine the quality of our Bible study are our attitude and our motivation. As we engage in Bible study, what should our attitude be? We must come to the Bible with a prayerful, respectful, open, responsive, ready-to-obey attitude (1 Cor. 2:14 to 3:3; John 7:17). We must keep in mind that the Book which we study is no ordinary book. This Book is God's Word to man! Thus, our response to the Bible is in reality a response to God, for *to respond to what he says is to respond to him.* Also, we must beware of pride or of any desire for self-enhancement through puffing up our knowledge (1 Cor. 8:1-2; 13:2). We should not be motivated to study the Bible so that we can be praised.

2

How the Holy Spirit Helps

In John 14:26 Jesus calls the Holy Spirit a "Helper" and says, "He will teach you all things." Some people would conclude that, since the Holy Spirit will teach us all things, Bible study is unnecessary. They would claim that we do not need to work at discovering the teachings of the Bible because the Holy Spirit will show us the truth directly. This raises an important question: *How* does the Holy Spirit help? *How* does the Holy Spirit teach? Does he help and teach me *directly* in such a way that I am inactive, merely a passive receiver of the truth? Or does he help and teach me *indirectly* in such a way that I am actively working at the discovery process with his help? There are at least six items to consider in resolving this problem.

First, to whom was John 14:26 spoken? The immediate context indicates that these words were spoken to people who were alive when Jesus was alive, people whom he lived with and spoke to (vv. 25-26). The larger context (John 13:1 to 18:1) narrows this down to Jesus' original disciples (excluding Judas). Thus, the promise "He will teach you all things" was made not to us, but to Jesus' original disciples. (And this promise *may* find its fulfillment in the inspiration of the New Testament writings through the disciples.) Even though we cannot claim John 14:26 as a promise given directly to us, on the basis of 1 Corinthians 2:12 it is reasonable to conclude that the Holy Spirit *can* teach *us* all things. But we are still left with the main question, *How* does the Holy Spirit teach us?

Second, if the Holy Spirit teaches me *directly* so that I am a passive receiver of the truth, why do I even need a Bible? If the Holy Spirit's pattern is to supply truth directly, then the Bereans should not have been commended by Luke for their study of the Old Testament (Acts 17:11). However, if the Holy Spirit's way of teaching us the truth includes our active use of the Bible, then, and *only then,* do we need a Bible. Thus, the mere fact that God has given us a Bible implies that God expects us to make active use of it.

Third, how does the Holy Spirit teach the gospel message in evangelism? The Holy Spirit will "convict the world concerning sin, and righteousness, and judgment" (John 16:8), but does he do so directly without using any instruments? No, the Holy Spirit uses the instrument of the human preacher (Rom. 10:14; 1 Cor. 3:6) and the instrument of the Word (Rom. 10:17; Acts 16:14). This does not prove, of course, that the Holy Spirit teaches the believer the same way he teaches the nonbeliever, but it does show that the Holy Spirit is not averse to working with human and verbal instruments. (It may appear at first glance that 1 John 2:27 indicates just the opposite of this when it says that "you have no need for anyone to teach you; but as His anointing teaches you about all things." However, the immediate context in verses 18-27 indicates that the word *anyone* in verse 27 refers mainly to the false-teaching antichrists, who wanted these early Christians to believe that Jesus is not the Messiah. Certainly none of these believers who already knew who Jesus is needed anyone to teach him such a lie. Thus, 1 John 2:27 is *not* stat-

ing that believers are taught spiritual truth directly
without the use of any instruments.)

Fourth, how did Jesus teach? Notice that the Holy
Spirit is likened to Jesus when he is referred to as "another Helper" who would be with the disciples forever
(John 14:16). The word *another* in the Greek means another helper *of the same sort* as Jesus. Thus, it is helpful
to note how Jesus taught, for there will probably be a
similarity between the way Jesus taught and the way
the Holy Spirit teaches. Jesus did not go around impart-
ing spiritual insight to passive minds. Those who
learned from Jesus had to observe his life and miracles,
ask and answer questions, enter into discussions with
other learners, and go through vivid experiences. Jesus
taught in such a way that his learners mentally were
very active. And when insight finally came from God (as
in Peter's declaration of Christ's identity, Matt.
16:16-17), it came after and was based on the various
active learning experiences through which the disciples had been guided. It is likely that the Holy Spirit
teaches in a similar manner. Perhaps this is why Jesus
said that the Holy Spirit would "guide" the original disciples into all truth (John 16:13). To be guided, the
learner must be active.

Fifth, how does God guide us in difficult situations?
How do we find out exactly what God wants us to do?
Does he directly give us the specific answer to our problem, or does he give us the ability to work out an
answer? Notice the wording of the promise, "if any of
you lacks wisdom" (the ability to work out a practical
answer), "let him ask God, . . . and it will be given him"
(Jas. 1:5). The pronoun "it" refers to "wisdom." Thus,
believers are told to ask, not for a direct answer from
God, but for wisdom. And what they receive is what they
ask for, wisdom to work out the answer with the help of

the Holy Spirit. This harmonizes completely with the biblical teaching regarding the use of our minds. We are to think hard and to reason logically, just the opposite of direct, intuitive insight given to passive receivers. (More is said about the use of the mind in chapter 13.)

Sixth, how am I to live the Christian life in general, actively or passively? If the Bible teaches that, on the whole, the Christian life is supposed to be passive, then we would expect the same to be true of learning spiritual truth, which is part of the Christian life.

Sometimes while seeking an answer to such a question, a person establishes a false twofold alternative in his mind. In this case, the problem is incorrectly posed, "Who does the spiritual things in my Christian life? Do I, or does God?"

I do it. | **God does it.**

In view of the warning not to try to live the Christian life or serve God in our own strength (John 15:4-5), we then conclude that the only alternative is to allow God to do it all while we do nothing.

The true picture, however, involves three alternatives, not merely two:

A	**B**	**C**
I do it.	**God and I do it together.**	**God does it.**
(I try to live and serve on my own without God's help.)	(I get my strength and direction from God, and then I do what he expects me to do, trusting in his help.)	(I am passive. I do nothing and expect God to do it all.)

The complete question which must be asked is, "Who does the spiritual things in my Christian life? Do I, or does God, or do we *both*?" While the Bible does tell us not to try to live and serve on our own, which eliminates alternative A, it also tells us to be active in our living and serving, which eliminates alternative C. Notice the active work mentioned in the following passages.

> I press on. (Phil. 3:12,14)
> Zealous for good deeds. (Titus 2:14)
> Created in Christ Jesus for good works.
> (Eph. 2:10)
> I will show you my faith by my works.
> (Jas. 2:18)

The only alternative which harmonizes with the biblical teaching on this matter is alternative B. (Keep in mind that at this point we are discussing how a Christian lives the Christian life, not how one *becomes* a Christian.)

Notice also that the Christian is not expected to be passively controlled by the Holy Spirit. The phrase "be filled with the Spirit" (Eph. 5:18) is, to be sure, in the passive voice. But the sentence goes on to state that the believer, once filled, is supposed to be quite active (v. 19 and following). In fact, the result of the Spirit's work in one's life is not his being passively controlled, but his "*self*-control" (Gal. 5:23, author's italics).

The New Testament repeatedly refers to God and the believer both working together. When Jesus says "apart from Me you can do nothing" (John 15:5), the strong implication is that *with Jesus you can* do it. Paul states, "I can do all things through Him who strengthens me" (Phil. 4:13), and "work out your salvation with fear and trembling; for it is God who is at work in you, both to will and to work for His good pleasure" (Phil. 2:12-13), and "be strong in the Lord . . . and having done everything, to stand firm" (Eph. 6:10-13). These passages show that when God gives us wisdom and strength, that very wisdom and strength become *ours!* We must use them, of course, never forgetting where we got them and never boasting as though we were self-sufficient. We must daily rely on God to direct us in, and strengthen us for, the work he wants *us* to do.

Thus, the Christian life is an active life, not a passive life, and there is no reason to believe that learning spiritual truth is done any differently. *If I want to learn spiritual truth, I must actively engage in the work of Bible study with the Holy Spirit's help.* I cannot expect the Holy Spirit to teach me biblical truth if I sit back and do nothing, but the Holy Spirit will teach me *as* I work hard at Bible study. There is nothing mystical about Bible study. When we pray, "Open my eyes, that I may behold/ Wonderful things from Thy law" (Ps. 119:18), we are not asking for direct revelation but for help as we actively search and ponder the Bible. Both are necessary: the Holy Spirit's help and teaching (illumination) and our diligent study. Paul indicated both aspects when he told Timothy to "Consider what I say, for the Lord will give you understanding in everything" (2 Tim. 2:7).

Part of that diligent study, a part which is often neglected, is to give careful attention to the matter of procedure. This is discussed in the next four chapters.

3

The Importance of Procedure

Very often the procedure used in solving a problem determines whether or not the answer is correct. The word *procedure* refers to the *way* a person goes about doing something, or *how* one arrives at his goal. Starting with a certain problem, *how* will he come up with the answer?

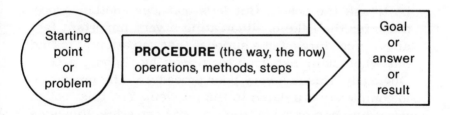

Procedure can make all the difference. Yet, procedure is seldom given enough careful attention. The examples in the following section illustrate these five facts about procedure:

1. Procedure makes the difference.
2. A poor procedure can give the correct answer.

3. Faulty assumptions can lead you astray.
4. Often the order of the steps in the procedure can alter the result.
5. A complete procedure is important.

Facts About Procedure Illustrated

Suppose your problem is to find the area of your garden (the number of square feet). You already know that your garden, which is rectangular in shape, measures 30 feet long and 20 feet wide. The procedure you use with these measurements will determine whether or not your answer is correct. If you multiply the length by the width, you will have the correct number of square feet. But if you use some other procedure or operation, such as addition, your answer will be incorrect. Procedure makes the difference.

Suppose your problem is to find out if your team won its last game. One of the most reliable procedures would be to ask the coach. But let's consider another procedure, for the sake of illustrating a very important fact about procedures. Let's suppose that you attempt to find out whether or not your team won by flipping a coin. Obviously, this is a very poor procedure. The procedure is completely unrelated to the problem. Yet, this foolish procedure can give you the correct answer! So this adds something new to our facts about procedure. On the one hand, a poor procedure can, and often does, give an incorrect answer. On the other hand, a poor procedure can give the correct answer. In some cases this is quite misleading. When the individual finds out that his answer is correct, he may feel that his procedure is dependable and will give him the correct answer the next time too. This can be a dangerous conclusion. A procedure which seems to have proven itself by producing the correct answer in one instance may be unduly trusted in following instances. If there is no opportunity to check the results, the individual may place undue confidence in those answers merely because he feels he has a reliable procedure. A procedure cannot be evaluated merely by checking the results which it produces in isolated instances. Procedures must also be evaluated in terms of their soundness and relevance to the problem situation. While it is safe to say that a procedure which gives an incorrect answer is a poor procedure, it is *not* safe to say that a procedure which gives the correct answer is necessarily a good procedure—because a poor procedure *can* give the correct answer.

Suppose your problem is to find out which of two neighbors likes to tinker with his car. As you observe both neighbors over several months, you notice that Mr. A spends a lot of time working on his car. Mr. B never does his own work. He always takes his car to the garage for repairs and adjustments. Your procedure is simply to observe the two men's activities. You conclude that Mr. A likes to tinker with his car, while Mr. B does not. Later, in chatting with these two neighbors, you discover that your answer is incorrect. Mr. A actually hates to work on his car, but he feels that he must save all the money he can by doing all of his own mechanical work. Mr. B actually loves to tinker with his car, but because of a busy schedule feels that he cannot spare the time. This second procedure (asking rather than merely observing) has produced a different answer. As in the previous example, the poor procedure could have produced the correct results if the circumstances of the situation had been different. But this example illustrates a new fact about procedure. The reason why the first procedure gave incorrect results is that a faulty assumption was involved. It was assumed that a person who likes something will spend more time doing it than a person who does not. If that assumption were correct, then observation would have been a good procedure. But the assumption failed to take the economic factor and the time factor into account, and thus the procedure that depended on that assumption turned out to be a poor procedure. Thus, when working out a procedure, it is extremely important to evaluate your assumptions. We automatically make assumptions in many cases: assumptions about what is average; assumptions about the reasons for certain behaviors; assumptions about a source's trustworthiness, etc. It is a very common mistake to make faulty assumptions, and this often happens because we do not consciously examine our assumptions. Again, procedure can make the difference, and our assumptions (which are employed in our procedures, or on which our procedures are based) can also make the difference.

Suppose your problem is to bake a cake "from scratch." Your procedure is spelled out for you on the recipe in front of you. If you do each step correctly, the result should be edible. If you do one or several steps incorrectly, the result would be less than edible, to say the least. It is helpful here to notice some additional facts about procedure which this example illustrates. The garden example dealt with a simple, one-step procedure, but here there are several steps in the overall procedure. When procedure becomes more complex (involving more steps or operations), the *order* and the *completeness* of the procedure become important. An out-of-order procedure (such as baking before mixing), or an incomplete procedure (such as forgetting to put in the flour) both produce a disappointing result. The order and completeness of the procedure are important.

This last example combines most of the facts we have

noticed about procedure so far. Suppose your problem is to find out whether or not a certain wooden box with a cover on it has anything in it. Your first method is simply to lift the box. When you lift it, it feels very heavy, so you decide that, yes, the box does have something in it. Then you try a second method, removing the cover. When you remove the cover you discover that there is nothing to be seen, so you decide that the box does not have anything in it after all. You notice that the box is lead-lined, which accounts for its heaviness when you lifted it. Then you try a third method, shaking the box. When you shake the box you hear something sliding from side to side. You examine the box closely and discover that it has a false bottom. When you remove the false bottom you find an envelope with a few important papers in it, and so you are finally aware that the box actually did have something in it from the start.

As we think about the three different methods which made up the procedure in this last example, we notice again the five facts about procedure. First, *procedure makes the difference.* Each time a different method was adopted an answer resulted which was different than the previous answer. Second, *a poor procedure can give the correct answer.* By lifting the box you decided that the answer to the problem was yes. (Of course, at that point you thought that what was in the box was something heavy, so even though your answer to the problem was correct your mental picture of the box's contents was very inaccurate.) Third, *faulty assumptions can lead you astray.* Here are the faulty assumptions which either did, or could have, led you astray in the above example. (1) If there is something in the box, it will be heavy enough for me to sense its presence by lifting the box. (2) The box itself is fairly light. (3) If anything is in the box, it will be visible when the cover is removed. (4) If anything is in the box, it is loose and will make some noise when the box is shaken. It takes only a moment's thought to realize that any one of these assumptions could be proven false by a particular type of box or by a particular type of content. The dangerous thing is, however, that *we all operate automatically on assumptions, and we must develop the mental discipline of consciously evaluating our assumptions.* Fourth, although order is not as crucial in this last example as it was in the cake example, *often the order of the steps in the procedure can alter the result.* Fifth, *a complete procedure is important.* The first two methods in this last example were not sufficient to arrive at a really satisfactory answer. In fact all three methods, in some circumstances (for instance, if the envelope had been wedged into place so it could not slide around), would still have been inadequate. Very often, single operations or single methods alone will be incomplete. A complete procedure will often involve many different types of methods or steps.

Facts About Procedure Applied to Bible Study

How do these five facts about procedure relate to personal Bible study?

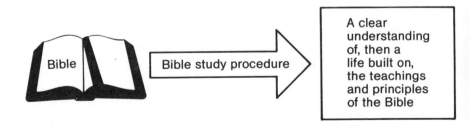

First, *procedure makes the difference.* Everyone who uses the Bible has a procedure, even though some people might not be aware of it, and others might deny it. Remember that the word *procedure* simply refers to the way you go about getting your answer, and everyone who uses the Bible uses it in some way or another. The way one person uses the Bible might be extremely simple, such as merely reading a passage. But that is still his procedure. Someone else might (with or without consciously thinking about his procedure) simply look up all the cross references given for a particular verse in the margin or at the foot of the page. That is his procedure. Someone else might (with or without consciously thinking about his procedure) simply outline a passage. That is his procedure. Someone might even say, "I have no procedure; I just ask the Holy Spirit to explain the words I read." But since that is the way he uses the Bible, that *is* his procedure.

Within each of the examples given at the beginning of this chapter, different answers resulted even though within each case the problem stayed the same. The starting point (the data, or materials, or sources) remained constant, but when different procedures were used, different answers resulted. The same holds true in Bible study. If you have three different people using three different procedures, even though they are all looking at the same Bible passage, they could come up with three different answers or three different interpretations. Part of the reason why we have so many different views of the same passage is because we have different procedures including different steps, different rules of interpretation, and different assumptions. Everyone uses a procedure, and different procedures can produce different results. Part of our responsibility as students of the Bible is to become aware of our procedure, evaluate it, and make sure we adopt a good procedure.

Second, *a poor procedure can give the correct answer.* Thus, it is not always easy to identify a poor procedure. A person who uses the procedure of merely reading the explanatory notes in his annotated Bible may find that quite often his "answer" agrees with his pastor's or his Sunday school teacher's answer, causing him to feel that he has come up with the correct answer. He will thus be encouraged to use this procedure again and again. However, this procedure and other similar procedures are very poor, even though at times they may in fact give the correct answer. Another poor procedure which is commonly used in topical study is the "proof text" method (having the "answer" already in mind and locating a verse which appears to support that answer). Of course, this procedure appears to give the "correct" answer simply because the person looking for proof texts favors those texts which fit his preconceived answer. (The reasons why these procedures are poor procedures are explained in the next two chapters.)

Third, *faulty assumptions can lead you astray.* You may assume, for instance, that the writer of a particular book of the Bible would express his theme by using certain words or phrases over and over again so that you can easily find out what the theme is by noting what words or phrases appear most often. Certainly this could be the case, but is it safe to assume that this procedure will lead you to the author's theme in every case? Could he express his theme in one way the first time he mentions it, and then, when he explains and illustrates it, use a varied vocabulary? Furthermore, is it safe to assume that every book of the Bible has a theme?

There is another category of assumptions which do not have to do with procedure (such as the procedure of looking for repeated words and phrases). Instead, these assumptions have to do with the actual content and conclusions. For instance, many people assume certain things about the nature of Christ, or about sin, etc. (The problem with such assumptions is also discussed in the next two chapters.)

Fourth, *often the order of the steps in the procedure can alter the result.* Some of the steps in Bible study procedure are necessary as preparations for other steps. For example, surveying an entire book must be done before an outline can be made. Respacing the text of a particular passage makes other steps which come later much easier, such as questioning the text or paraphrasing the text. In a topical study, sorting (classifying passages) should precede close scrutiny of the key passages. These and many other aspects of Bible study are best done in a particular sequence. It is important to pay close attention to the order of the steps you use in Bible study. That is why chapters 17 and 18 are laid out as a step-by-step procedure, to help you accomplish each step at the best time in the sequence.

Fifth, *a complete procedure is important.* Each different step or operation in the overall Bible study procedure makes its own unique contribution. The more complete your procedure, the more confidence you can have in your results. The more steps or operations you omit, the more likely it is that you have not discovered all that you need to know about the passage in order to make a sound interpretation. The procedures in chapters 17 and 18 are designed to be as complete as possible without being unnecessarily repetitious.

In a nutshell: *In personal Bible study you should follow a correct and complete procedure step by step in proper order and consciously beware of misleading assumptions.*

Confidence in Your Procedure

We have a reliable Bible. It is the Word of God. But it is not enough merely to have a reliable Bible. If we are to have confidence in the biblical teachings which we believe and in the biblical principles by which we live, *we must also have a reliable way of deriving those teachings and principles from the Bible. We must have confidence in our study procedure if we are to have confidence in the results of that procedure.* The person who does not pay close and critical attention to his Bible study procedure has a very flimsy foundation under his own beliefs, and he has no right to recommend those beliefs to anyone else. The apostle Peter spoke of the tragic outcome of holding incorrect beliefs or interpretations when he stated that people who distort the Scriptures do so "to their own destruction" (2 Pet. 3:16).

Do you have confidence in your present Bible study procedure? Are you willing to try Direct Bible Discovery?

4

The Direct Procedure

The name *Direct Bible Discovery* is carefully chosen to call attention to two fundamental aspects of this approach to personal Bible study. The first fundamental aspect is the *direct* or *independent* aspect, which is discussed in this chapter. The second fundamental aspect is the *discovery* or *inductive* aspect, which is discussed in the next chapter.

If you want to find out something about a Bible book or a Bible topic, where should you go? The best place to go,

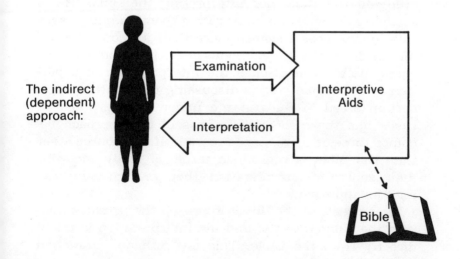

The indirect (dependent) approach:

Examination

Interpretive Aids

Interpretation

Bible

of course, is *directly* to the Bible itself. But many people do not go to the Bible to find out what the Bible says! Instead, they go to books and other sources *about* the Bible. Their approach to the Bible is *indirect.*

The approach illustrated on page 37 is called the indirect approach simply because the person does not go directly to the Bible. He goes to the Bible indirectly through interpretive aids. Interpretive aids include annotated Bibles, Bible commentaries, Bible dictionaries, Christian tapes, and local authorities such as the pastor, Sunday School teacher, or seminary or Bible college professor. In other words, rather than examining the biblical text itself, one examines books and other sources *about* the Bible. The only times when he directly contacts the Bible in this approach is when the Bible is quoted in the aid, or when he bothers to check up on the aid by reading the passage in his own Bible. Notice also that the interpretation which he comes up with is taken primarily from the interpretive aids and only indirectly from the Bible itself. Thus he is neither studying the Bible nor interpreting the Bible. He is studying the aids and interpreting them! In many cases this indirectness becomes more than just one step removed from the Bible. Sometimes, for instance, one commentator will discuss the interpretation of a particular theologian who is discussing the relevance of a certain creed to the passage under consideration. In cases like these the indirectness of the approach becomes three or more steps removed. If any source other than the Bible is your main target of study and your main source of interpretation, then you are using the indirect approach.

In contrast, in the direct approach the person examines the Bible directly, and his interpretation is taken directly from the Bible. This is firsthand interaction with the Bible. The person studies the Bible largely independent of other sources about the Bible. It is like seeing the parade with your own eyes rather than seeing a videotape of parts of the parade on a news broadcast. It is like feeding yourself rather than being fed by someone else.

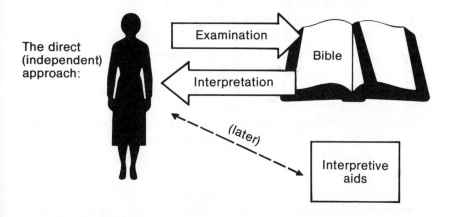

This emphasis on going directly to the Bible is not meant to minimize the value of interpretive aids. Actually, interpretive aids have a very important place in personal Bible study. Commentaries and the like can be very helpful. For example, they can provide important background information on a book of the Bible, a location, a historical event, a linguistic fact, a custom, etc. They can also be used to compare the commentator's interpretation of a particular passage with the interpretation you have already arrived at directly from the Bible.

You should remember that interpretive aids serve their purpose best when they are used *as aids*. You should focus your primary attention in the Bible and not become *dependent* upon commentaries and other interpretive aids. At the same time, do not neglect the wealth of facts and ideas than can be found in the aids. After you have arrived at your own interpretation from your own direct study of the biblical text, it is wise to compare your interpretation with the interpretations of others. Read whatever interpretive aids are appropriate and give full consideration to their viewpoints and interpretations. These aids may point out a fact from the text which you had missed, or a way of putting the facts together which you had not considered. When you find that someone else's interpretation differs from your own, it should drive you right back to the Bible for more direct study and contemplation. In this way interpretive aids can perform a very valuable service for you, so long as you do not become dependent on them and do not use them as a crutch or as a substitute for your own direct Bible study.

It is very unfortunate that many people think of the Bible as having an aura of mystery around it. This mindset about the Bible makes a person believe that he cannot approach it or understand it. However, the Bible was not written to hide information or to create mysteries. The Bible was written so that we could know about God and about ourselves. Many passages throughout the Bible indicate clearly that the Bible is to be read, understood, and responded to.

> You shall read this law in front of all Israel in their hearing. . . . that they may hear and learn and fear the Lord your God, and be careful to observe all the words of this law. And their children . . . will hear and learn to fear the Lord your God. (Deut. 31:11-13)

These have been written that you may believe.
(John 20:31)

We write nothing else to you than what you read and
understand. (2 Cor. 1:13)

There are many more passages throughout the Bible
where the same idea is stated. The Bible is to be read and
understood. (It may appear at first glance that 2 Peter
1:20 teaches just the opposite of this when it says that
"no prophecy of Scripture is a matter of one's own interpretation." However, the immediate context in
verses 16-21 shows that Peter is actually explaining the
source of the prophecies. Verse 20 is speaking about
how each prophecy originated, not about how to interpret the prophecy after it is written. Notice, in the immediate context, the repeated mention of the prophecies'
divine source as opposed to a human source. The point of
verses 20-21 is that no scriptural prophecy ever came
into being by the clever work of the prophet in either
interpreting events or predicting history. Instead, God
was the source of the prophet's message. The Holy
Spirit moved each prophet to say what he said. Thus, 2
Peter 1:20 does *not* contradict the idea that the Bible is
for us to read and understand.)

There are, of course, some places in the Bible which,
although they *can* be understood, are not understood
easily (2 Pet. 3:16; Acts 8:30-31). But even such difficult
portions should not discourage us from engaging in
direct Bible study. They challenge us to even more intense direct Bible study.

One very common problem with the indirect approach
is that the person is often dependent on (perhaps even
becomes addicted to) the use of the interpretive aids. He
may feel that he cannot do Bible study without them.

And this unfortunate feeling of dependence is heightened both when the person is a new Christian and when the person is confronted with the archaic language of the King James Version of the Bible. (More is said about translations in chapter 16.) When any person becomes dependent on the aids, then the aids are no longer aids at all, but they become all important and actually take the place of the Bible as the main object of study and the main source of the person's interpretations.

Another serious problem with the indirect approach has to do with the selection of the interpretive aids. How do you know a good commentary from a bad one? In the final analysis, every commentary, every annotated Bible, every teaching from your pastor, every Bible dictionary, must be evaluated in terms of its fidelity to the Bible. In other words, if you do not go directly to the Bible and check every human interpreter, you have no firm basis for choosing one interpretation instead of another, one commentary instead of another. All you have is the opinions of others.

Not all Bible study aids are equally interpretive, however. Some are more interpretive than others, and some are not interpretive at all. Compare the various types of aids on the chart on the next page. Noninterpretive aids are aids which are not designed to interpret any Bible passages. They are very valuable in personal Bible study, and you should not hesitate to use them often throughout your entire Bible study procedure. (More is said about each of the noninterpretive aids in chapter 16.) Interpretive aids are aids which are designed to give at least some interpretation of the Bible passage. Again, they are very valuable, but they need to be used wisely. (Their use is discussed more in chapters 17 and 18.)

Notice the example of the Bereans. After Paul preached to these Jews they were "examining the Scrip-

BIBLE STUDY AIDS
(for studying the English Bible)

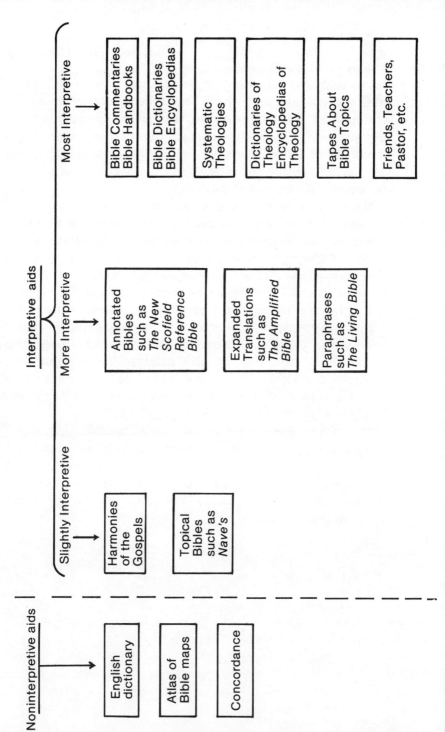

Noninterpretive aids

- English dictionary
- Atlas of Bible maps
- Concordance

Interpretive aids

Slightly Interpretive

- Harmonies of the Gospels
- Topical Bibles such as *Nave's*

More Interpretive

- Annotated Bibles such as *The New Scofield Reference Bible*
- Expanded Translations such as *The Amplified Bible*
- Paraphrases such as *The Living Bible*

Most Interpretive

- Bible Commentaries Bible Handbooks
- Bible Dictionaries Bible Encyclopedias
- Systematic Theologies
- Dictionaries of Theology Encyclopedias of Theology
- Tapes About Bible Topics
- Friends, Teachers, Pastor, etc.

tures daily, to see whether these things were so." They
did not merely ask their rabbi or a scribe what he
thought of Paul's message; they went directly to the
Scriptures. It is especially significant that Luke labels
such direct Bible study as being "noble-minded" (Acts
17:11). The Bible repeatedly invites and encourages us
to come and examine it directly.

If you are a pastor or teacher, encourage your congre-
gation or your class to check up on you by evaluating
what you say according to their own direct study of the
Bible. If they get their information firsthand, they will
be more sure of their convictions (John 4:42; 2 Chron.
9:5-6) and will have a greater appreciation of your teaching ministry. Many pastors and teachers, without attempting to, actually encourage dependence on themselves and other "authorities" which, in the long run,
discourages the individual Christian from going directly to the Bible. If a person does not know how to go
about direct Bible discovery, consider it your responsibility to show him how. (See Appendix E.)

If you are a church member, class member, or seminary or college student, you should gain all you can from
your pastor or teacher, but you should also examine the
Scriptures, as the Bereans did, to see if what you are
hearing is true to the Bible. You should form a lifelong
habit of going directly to the Bible.

5

The Discovery Procedure

What should be your purpose for going directly to the Bible? The best purpose, of course, is to find out what the Bible says—to *discover* the meaning of the biblical text. But many people, when they go to the Bible, do not find out what the Bible says! They do not get the meaning *out of* the text. Instead, they read a meaning *into* the text. This is done when a person assumes certain beliefs or views to be true, and then as he goes to the biblical text he goes in order to *verify* (find support for) those assumptions, and/or he *interprets the text on the basis of those assumptions.* The danger lies in the fact that this process of reading meaning into the text often goes on *without the person being aware* that he is doing it. Thus, he may think he is discovering what the Bible says, whereas he is merely extending his own assumptions.

The idea of discovery, as opposed to extending assumptions, is parallel to the idea of *induction,* as opposed to *deduction* (terms which are more commonly used in the fields of logic and science). A brief look at induction and deduction will help explain what is meant by *discovery* and *extending assumptions.*

The terms *induction* and *deduction* describe two opposite reasoning processes. Induction is a process in which a person begins with specific, individual items (facts, instances, observations, etc.) and puts them together to form a general principle.

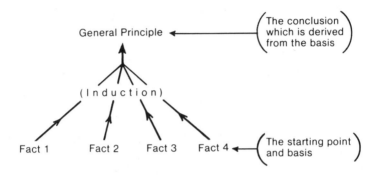

He observes the particulars and then, upon thinking how they relate to each other and how they fit together, formulates a general principle or law which summarizes all the individual facts. In induction, thought always moves from the particular to the general.

In deduction, thought moves in the opposite direction, from general to particular. Deduction is a process in which a person begins with a general principle and applies it to one or several specific instances. He assumes, or adopts, the general principle (or law, or premise) and then infers something about each instance either by interpreting each particular instance in light of the general principle or by predicting what will be the case in each particular instance based on the general principle.

Here is an example of induction and deduction. Imagine that you are the world's first metallurgist. You are interested in the physical properties of various metals. One day you observe that when copper is heated it expands slightly. This is fact 1. Later you observe that iron also expands when heated. This is fact 2. Now you begin to wonder if this could also be true of other metals, so you experiment with magnesium, lead, zinc, barium, nickel, and vanadium. Your experiments yield the information that each of these metals also expands when heated. So you now have eight facts which you can compare. With these eight individual facts in mind you sum-

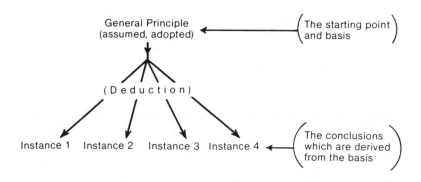

marize them and state a general law, "Metals expand when heated." Your thinking process has moved from the facts to the general law. The law is based on the individual facts. You have used an *inductive* reasoning process. But now you want to apply this new law to other instances. With the general law in mind you are now able to predict what will happen with other metals which you have not tested. You can now say, "Metals expand when heated. Platinum is a metal; thus platinum will expand when heated." Now your thinking process has moved from the general law to the individual instance. The inference about platinum is based on the general law. You have used a *deductive* reasoning process. (This last pattern of reasoning is also called a "syllogism.")

Here is another example of induction and deduction.

Members of a jury, with open minds, begin by listening to item after item of testimony and evidence. After thinking about how all these individual facts fit together, the jury infers that the defendant is innocent. This general conclusion is based on and derived from the particular facts in the case. However, if the jury began by assuming that the defendant was guilty, when they heard the testimonies and the evidence they would apply that premise (that the defendant is guilty) and interpret each individual item of testimony or evidence in light of that premise. Thus, the jury would deduce things about each item of evidence based on and derived from the assumed premise. It is obvious that such deductive reasoning would do a terrible injustice to some of the evidence by causing them to interpret it incorrectly. Because a general principle or general viewpoint was assumed (adopted without an adequate basis for its adoption), the facts would be obscured and the real truth never discovered.

Discovery in Bible study is very similar to induction as described above. The following diagrams illustrate the *extending assumptions* approach to the Bible and the *discovery* approach to the Bible.

The approach illustrated on page 49 is called the *extending-assumptions* approach because the assumptions which the person has before he goes to the Bible are (often unconsciously) carried with him to the Bible and applied to (extended into) the biblical text. As he "reads" the passage with certain ideas already in mind, he may not see all that there is to see in the passage. (This is much like the vacationer who did not see the detour sign because all he had on his mind was his need of sleep, and he was intently looking for motel signs.) Or he may interpret the text in such a way that it appears to support his assumptions. (This process of reading

Before Bible study   **During Bible study**

The
Extending-
Assumptions
(deductive)
Approach:

2.
One (often uncon-
sciously) brings
these ideas and
views to the text.

1.
One already has
assumptions, gen-
eralizations, views,
etc.

3.
One then interprets
the specific state-
ments of the Bible
in the light of
prior ideas. One
reads meaning into
the text, or looks
for support for prior
assumptions.

meaning into the text is also known as eisegesis.)

This same error often occurs when a person incorrectly uses proof texts. The text which he cites is supposed to prove his point, whereas in reality it *may* be
only part of the scriptural evidence which relates to the
issue, or it may be interpreted by him in such a way as to
agree with his assumption. In either case the assumption is the basis for the selection of the verse or for the
interpretation of the verse, and the verse is then cited to
prove the conclusion, which is the same as, or similar to,
the assumption. This is a pure case of circular reasoning (also called "begging the question").

This deductive process *often goes on without the per-*

son being aware that he is using a deductive reasoning process, or that he is violating the text by reading meaning into it rather than allowing the text to give out its own inherent meaning. Furthermore, making unfounded assumptions is so widespread that it would appear to be an automatic human tendency. In fact, the New Testament records several cases in which individuals or groups made such assumptions (Luke 2:42-44; 3:23; Acts 2:15; 7:22-25; 14:19-20; 16:27; 21:27-29).

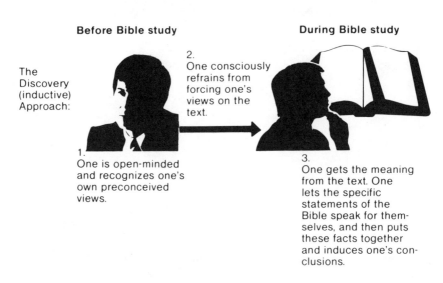

The Discovery (inductive) Approach:

Before Bible study

1. One is open-minded and recognizes one's own preconceived views.

2. One consciously refrains from forcing one's views on the text.

During Bible study

3. One gets the meaning from the text. One lets the specific statements of the Bible speak for themselves, and then puts these facts together and induces one's conclusions.

In contrast, in the discovery approach the person recognizes that he has views, beliefs, and prejudices, but he also realizes that he cannot force these ideas on the Bible. So when he goes to the Bible he is very careful to temporarily set his assumptions aside to be evaluated later.

Of course, no one can completely set aside all of his assumptions. In the first place, there are certain unconscious assumptions everyone must make about the reliability of his senses and his reasoning processes just to be able to read and think. In the second place, even those conscious assumptions about specific doctrines or certain passages can never be completely dismissed. No one can be totally objective. Yet, the goal is to become as objective as possible. Thus, during Bible study the person using the discovery approach very carefully and objectively examines the specific statements of the text. He then thinks about how they relate to each other and how they fit together and he formulates his conclusions on the basis of the text, rather than interpreting the text in light of his assumptions. (The various rules and principles which should be used in the actual interpretation of the text are discussed in chapters 10 through 13.)

By using an inductive process he discovers the real meaning of the biblical text. He lets the Bible speak for itself. He gets the meaning out of the text rather than reading a meaning into the text. (This process of getting the meaning out of the text is also known as exegesis.) Then, and only then, can he evaluate his prior assumptions.

Even such a "sacred" thing as a doctrinal statement must not be imposed on the Bible. After all, a doctrinal statement, or church creed (no matter how historic) is a human product. No doctrinal statement is inspired. Only the Bible is inspired. It may well be that your doctrinal statement is, in fact, correct. And if it is correct, you have nothing to lose and everything to gain by temporarily setting it aside while you let the Bible speak for itself. When you have formulated your conclusions through a discovery process you will then learn that your findings do support your doctrinal statement. Thus you have gained valid support for your doctrinal statement. However, if your doctrinal statement is incorrect, you will not find that out if you use an extending-assumptions approach, because the conclusions arrived at in such a process will automatically appear to support the doctrinal statement that was assumed. The biblical evidence will be selectively chosen, and/or passages will be interpreted in light of the assumed doctrinal statement. The only way to find out if your doctrinal statement is incorrect is to use the discovery approach.

The discovery (inductive) process requires an open mind. It is unfortunate, however, that the term "open-minded" is often misused and often misunderstood. On the one hand, some people think that being open-minded is the worst thing in the world because they think that an open-minded person is either gullible or is wishy-washy and without any convictions. On the other hand, other people think that being open-minded is the best thing in the world because they are against prejudice, bigotry, and intolerance. However, both of these viewpoints are overreactions. The best condition is when a person is open-minded until he has objectively examined all the relevant facts and has reflectively considered various possible ways to put those facts together to form a conclusion. If he has been open-minded in his research and reasoning, then he has every right to firmly hold to his conclusions as definite convictions. The problems arise (1) when a person starts the process with a closed mind and thus never really examines the facts or the alternate ways of putting the facts together, or (2) when a person ends the process with an open mind when the facts in the case actually call for a definite conclusion. Having a closed mind is not a problem in itself. The problem is in having a closed mind too soon in the process. Likewise, having an open mind is not a problem in itself. The problem is in retaining an open mind when the facts and the possible alternatives have demanded a conclusion (and in many cases, a personal commitment).

Just as any jury with a closed mind never really sees the evidence as it is, and thus seldom arrives at the truth, so a Bible student who begins with a closed mind never really sees the biblical text as it is, and thus seldom arrives at the true teachings and principles of the Bible. We must constantly beware of extending our unfounded assumptions. We must constantly examine the biblical text with an open mind to discover its meaning.

Again notice the example of the Bereans. After Paul preached to these Jews, they were "examining the Scriptures daily, to see whether these things were so" (Acts 17:11). They were not gullible, for they did not blindly accept Paul's message. Nor were they closedminded, for they gave Paul's message a fair hearing. Then they went to the Scriptures to objectively examine the statements of the Scriptures without imposing their own prior viewpoint *or* Paul's new viewpoint on them. They let the Scriptures speak for themselves. They discovered what the Scriptures said. Then many of them evaluated Paul's conclusion as being the correct one, for they too then believed (v. 12).

In a nutshell: Go directly to the biblical text with an open mind and let it speak for itself so that you can discover its true meaning.

6

The Order of the Elements

Bible study serves as the link between the Bible and the use of the Bible (application and service), as illustrated in the diagram on the next page. Not only are all of the twelve elements important, but their order is also important.

The Holy Spirit inspired each book of the Bible as it was originally written so that its contents would be completely reliable. Most of the Old Testament books were originally written in Hebrew, and the New Testament books were written in Greek. The Holy Spirit also preserved those writings (the word *Scriptures* means simply "writings"). He guided the believers both before and after Christ in their recognition of the inspired writings and in their rejection of other uninspired writings, so that only inspired writings were included in the canon (the list of inspired books). And even though we do not have any of the original manuscripts today, many ancient copies of those original manuscripts have been preserved for us. Specialists in textual criticism compare these copies to determine which wordings most accurately represent the original manuscripts. (Textual criticism is also called lower criticism and is not to be confused with higher criticism.) The Hebrew Old Testament and the Greek New Testament which result are thus remarkably close to the wording of the originals.

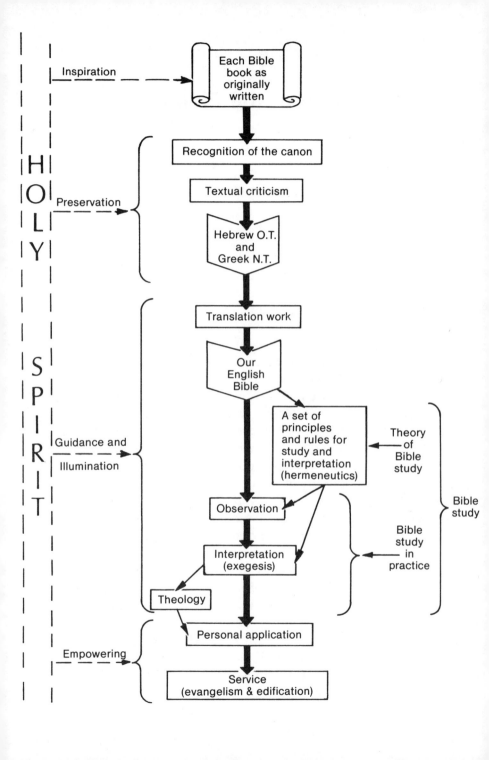

The Holy Spirit further guides men as they translate the Hebrew and Greek to give us our English Bible today. (More is said about translation in chapter 16.)

The above paragraph briefly describes the stages in the production of our English Bible. The ministry of the Holy Spirit is not finished, however, merely in the production of a Bible for us to study. The Holy Spirit continues to work as we study, apply, and share the Bible. When a person actually practices Bible study he will follow a certain procedure, either consciously or unconsciously, based on a set of principles and rules (hermeneutics) for Bible study and interpretation. This set of principles and rules is derived initially from one's common way of reading any piece of literature, and then is modified as he observes what the Bible itself indicates about how it is to be interpreted. (More about these principles of interpretation is discussed in chapters 10 through 13.) The theory of Bible study then becomes Bible study in actual practice as the person first observes what the biblical text says, then interprets it, and then integrates his interpretations into a systematic statement of the Bible's teachings known as theology. The Holy Spirit's ministry of illumination applies to each of these elements of Bible study. Then the Holy Spirit empowers the person to apply those teachings in his life and to share and exemplify those teachings with both non-Christians (evangelism) and Christians (edification).

There are three elements in the practice of Bible study which are often taken out of order: *observation, interpretation,* and *application.* Personal application should come only after you are certain that your interpretation is sound. An incorrect interpretation applied to one's life can have tragic results. Thus, any so-called devotional approach to the Bible which stresses application to the neglect of sound interpretation is actually quite dangerous. Also, one's interpretation must be based on thoughtful, thorough, and intense observation. You need to know precisely what the text says (and what it does not say) before you try to determine what the text means. Thus, the logical order of these three elements should always be: first observation, then interpretation, then application.

In a nutshell: Go directly to the biblical text and carefully observe what it says. Then interpret its meaning, apply it in your life, and share it with someone else.

7

Observation

Systematic observation is the first and most basic phase in the actual practice of personal Bible study. Many times a person has a lot of trouble figuring out what a Bible passage *means* because he has not first done the work of carefully and objectively observing exactly what the passage *says.*

An observation is a statement regarding what the biblical text actually says, how it says it, and what it omits. An observation is *not* an interpretation. An observation has to do with the factual. An interpretation has to do with the meaning and significance of the factual. Notice the distinction between observation and interpretation in the chart on the following page.

It is very easy (and very common) for a person to claim that he observed something, when in reality he both observed *and* interpreted it. Very frequently we confuse the observation phase with the interpretation phase, as in the following instances.

You see a family pack a lot of camping equipment into a car and then drive away. You may think that you "observed" them leaving on a camping trip, but that is not what you observed at all. The interpretation about leaving on a camping trip comes from inside your own head, based on an assumption. All you actually observed was a family packing a lot of camping equipment into a car and

An observation states

—an isolated *fact,* or

—a *relationship* between facts, or

—a *pattern* of relationships between facts

---

which is indicated directly by the biblical text. It is something which is concrete, explicit, evident, visible, and easily verifiable, in the text. (An observation can also be a statement of what the text omits.) An observation states with complete certainty what the text says.

An interpretation states

—an *explanation* of the *meaning* or intent of

—or a *summary* of, or a *generalization* based on

—or a *principle* derived from

—or the *significance* of

—or a *conclusion,* or an *implication,* or an *inference* drawn from

—or a *judgment* about

---

those facts, relationships, or patterns.

This interpretation is not found explicitly in the text, but it *must be based on (induced from) observations.* An interpretation states with varying degrees of certainty what the text means. An interpretation is not an application.

then driving away. You have confused observation with interpretation. Actually they were taking the equipment to the home of a relative who was borrowing it for the next week.

You see a man carrying a guitar case. You may think that you "observed" a musician with his instrument, but again that is your interpretation, not your observation. What you actually observed was a man carrying a guitar case. You have assumed that there is a guitar in the case, and you have assumed that people carrying instruments can play them. Actually, he is a very nonmusical father who has picked up a case for his daughter's guitar at the music store.

Most misjudgments or misinterpretations in everyday experience are due to our failure to observe carefully, and to our failure to keep our judgments or interpretations from being built on our assumptions rather than our observations.

Making observations on a passage in the Bible is much the same as making observations on a real-life incident. However, one difference is that a biblical passage may state an interpretation of its own (for example, Eccl. 12:13-14; Matt. 7:12) or some generalization or principle (for example, Rom. 3:10-12; Col. 3:23; John 3:36; 1 Thess. 5:18). In this case, when you restate that interpretation, generalization, or principle you are merely making an observation, not an interpretation, since you are merely stating something which is indicated directly by the text. Later you may observe some relationship between this general principle and some other items in the text and then infer another generalization from those observations. But as long as an interpretation is explicitly stated in the text, your restatement of it is an observation rather than an interpretation.

Even though this distinction between observation of what the text says and interpretation of what the text means is stressed here, it should *not* be thought that the text does not mean what it says. Often, what the text says may not need any further interpretation in order to make good sense, since its meaning is quite evident in what it says. In other words, *usually a passage will say exactly what it means and will mean exactly what it says. Yet, there will often be additional significance and additional inference beyond what the passage explicitly says. This is the point at which the distinction between observation and interpretation comes into play.*

For example, Acts 16:6-10 is explicitly about Paul's trip from present-day western Turkey to Macedonia. The passage means what it says about where Paul went. However, there is more meaning inherent in the passage than what is evident on the surface. Although the passage is not explicitly about divine guidance, it gives some very interesting insights into how God directed Paul and how he may direct us as well. Notice that the call to preach in Macedonia followed two negative commands. God led Paul one step at a time, rather than revealing his future plans too far ahead of time. The point is that this interpretation about God's leading is *not* expressly stated in the passage, yet it is based on observations of things that *are* expressly stated in the passage. Thus, the passage says what it means and means what it says about Paul's trip to Macedonia. No further interpretation regarding where Paul went is needed, and when you note where Paul went you are making an observation. However, when you note how God led Paul, that is an interpretation, since you have to put several explicit statements together in order to infer that interpretation.

All too often, when dealing with a Bible passage, we confuse the observation phase with the interpretation phase. We fail to make careful observation of the text first, so that we are thoroughly familiar with exactly what the text says, how it says it, and what it does not say. For example, what does the well-known nursery rhyme below say? Does it say that a child named Mary had a lamb that went with her every time she went somewhere?

> Mary had a little lamb,
> Its fleece was white as snow,

And everywhere that Mary went
The lamb was sure to go.

He followed her to school one day—
That was against the rule.
It made the children laugh and play
To see a lamb at school.

And so the teacher turned him out,
But still he lingered near;
And waited patiently about
Till Mary did appear;

. . . .

What makes the lamb love Mary so?"
The eager children cry;
"Oh, Mary loves the lamb, you
know,"
The teacher did reply.

According to what the text of this rhyme actually says, we really do not know how old Mary was. Nor do we really know how often the lamb went *with* Mary, if ever! When we make a careful distinction between observation and interpretation, we can see that some of our assumptions may be unfounded.

Observations	Resultant Interpretations and Questions
1. The rhyme does not give Mary's age.	1. Any age will harmonize with the rhyme: a. Mary *could* have been a school age child. b. Mary *could have been a mother.* c. *Mary could* have been a grandmother.
2. The rhyme does not say	2. *Perhaps* the lamb had a habit of sniffing out Mary's trail and thus

that the lamb ever went *with* Mary.

3. Compare:
"*everywhere* that Mary went"
"It followed her to school *one day*"

following her path "everywhere" she went.

3. Is this a contradiction? (Of course, the rhyme does *not* say that the lamb followed Mary to school *only* one day. However, it is very likely that the lamb did follow Mary to school only one day, or a few days at most, since line 5 could hardly mean "as usual," and since the author could have easily substituted "each day" for "one day" if that had been the intent.) What about all the other days Mary went to school? Or did Mary (who could have been a parent or grandparent) go to school only one day?

Perhaps the word *everywhere,* as it is used in this context, means something other than absolutely-every-place-with-absolutely-no-exceptions. "Everywhere" could be used in the sense that the lamb had been every place (at least once) that Mary had been. Or (and this is most likely the *intent* of the author's use of the word "everywhere") it *could* be used merely in the sense that the lamb followed Mary very often when Mary went to a wide variety of places.

No matter what the traditional interpretation of the nursery rhyme might be, it *is* a rather vague rhyme. It just does not say all that we traditionally assume that it says. An attempt has been made here to observe care-

fully exactly what the rhyme actually says, and to consider various possible ways of putting the evidence of
the text together. But since the evidence does not de-
mand one interpretation above the others in the three
issues raised, no dogmatic interpretations are given
above.

It may seem ridiculous, and perhaps rightly so, to
scrutinize a nursery rhyme so closely. Yet, this sort of
scrutiny is necessary, especially when we examine biblical texts. This little exercise with Mary and her lamb
illustrates two errors which are quite common in Bible
study. The first error is that of getting more out of the
text than is actually there by reading certain ideas into
the text based on assumptions (see John 21:22-23). As a
general rule, the fewer assumptions you extend into the
text, the fewer dogmatic interpretations you will make,
other factors being equal. The second error is that of
failing to appreciate the *intent* of the writer by failing to
integrate all of the text's evidence to help you arrive at a
meaningful understanding of the writer's actual
thought.

8

Sample Observations

This chapter provides a few sample observations on Mark 2:1-12. These samples will have much more value to you if you study the passage quoted on page 69 and then write out some of your own observations before reading the samples. At this point, write out *only* observations. You should set aside at least one hour to study the passage and write out your own observations. As you do so, keep the following in mind:

1. Keep the distinction between observation and interpretation clearly in mind.

2. Do not try to make striking observations. Concentrate your efforts on being accurate rather than on being spectacular.

3. Do not bother to write out observations on the mechanics of the English text. Of course, for those who are able to study the Bible in the original languages, that is by far the best. But if you study the Bible in an English translation, your Bible study can still be very meaningful and rewarding. However, you should be aware of some aspects of the English translation which are not in the original manuscripts. For instance, the earliest known manuscripts of the New Testament books were written entirely in letters the same size without spaces between the words, without our modern English type of punctuation, without paragraphs, without quotation

marks, and without chapter and verse divisions. Thus, the translators and editors must supply all of these as they feel they best fit their understanding of the text. (The chapter divisions which appear in our present Bibles were added to the text in 1228, the verse divisions in 1551.) It is not wise to base your interpretation of a passage solely on such things as capitalization of a certain word, punctuation, sentence and paragraph divisions, quotation marks, or verse or chapter divisions. Do not waste your time making observations of such aspects of the English translation. Such observations are pointless because they do not come to us from the original manuscripts. Thus, they form a flimsy basis for interpretations. There are also some superficial aspects of the English text which you should not waste your time observing. For instance, the longest or shortest word in a passage, the longest or shortest sentence, the middle sentence of a paragraph or the middle word of a sentence, etc., are all merely mechanical aspects which are unique to the English text. Avoid making observations on these aspects also. They are pointless.

4. Focus your efforts on writing out observations of *relationships* between facts and *patterns* of relationships. Do not be satisfied merely to write out isolated facts which would be obvious to any reader at first glance. (In reference to the Mark 2:1-12 passage, such obvious observations might include, "This happened in Capernaum," or "There was a crowd there," or "Jesus healed the paralytic.") Naturally, you will observe such things easily the first time you read the passage. Since these facts are so easily accessible, you may not even need to write them down. Later, of course, such obvious aspects of the text may be brought together with your other observations to help form the basis for some of your interpretations. Your interpretations will be based

on *all* you know about the passage, both the obvious
(which you may not have written out) and the not-so-
obvious (which you have written out). The majority of
your observations should be observations of relationships and patterns, not merely isolated facts.

The text of Mark 2:1-12 which follows is respaced.
(The reason for respacing a text is explained in chapter
17.)

The purpose at this point is not to try to be exhaustive,
but only to illustrate a few observations and some possible interpretations based on those observations.

Mark 2:1-12

Verse

1   And when He had come back to Capernaum
                    several days afterward,
          it was heard that He was at home.

2   And many were gathered together,
                    so there was no longer room,
                              even near the door;
          and He was speaking the word to them.

3 And they came,
                    bringing to Him a paralytic,
                              carried by four men.

4   And being unable to get to Him
                    on account of the crowd,
          they removed the roof above Him;
              and when they had dug an opening,
          they let down the pallet on which the paralytic was lying.

5   seeing their faith
      And Jesus   said to the paralytic,
                    "My son, your sins are forgiven."

6 But there were some of the scribes sitting there
                    and reasoning in their hearts,

7   "Why does this man speak that way?
                     He is blaspheming;
                     who can forgive sins but God alone?"

8   And immediately

                        ╱ in His Spirit
        Jesus, perceiving   that they were reasoning that way
             ┊   within themselves,
        said to them,
            "Why are you reasoning about these things
                        in your hearts?
9   Which is easier,
            to say to the paralytic, 'Your sins are forgiven;'
            or to say, 'Arise, and take up your pallet and walk'?
10   But in order that you may know   ╱on earth
            that the Son of man has authority   to forgive sins"—
        He said to the paralytic,—
11   "I say to you, rise, take up your pallet and go home."
12   And he rose
            and immediately took up the pallet
                    and went out in the sight of all;
            so that they were all amazed
                and were glorifying God,
                    saying, "We have never seen anything like this."

Observations on Mark 2:1-12

1. Jesus sees *their* (plural) faith, yet he responds by addressing just one man, the paralytic (v. 5).

2. The passage does not say why the paralytic was brought to Jesus, and no words of the paralytic are recorded (entire passage).

3. The paralytic obviously needed physical healing, but Jesus forgave his sins first (vv. 3-5).

4. Jesus' question to the scribes was not "Which is easier to *do*?" (forgive or heal), but "Which is easier to *say* . . .?" (v. 9). Also, Jesus' question to the scribes con-

trasted something that could *not* be checked (saying "your sins are forgiven") with something that could be checked (saying "arise . . .") (v. 9).

5. The labels for inner functions differ from our customary usage. We often say that thinking is in the head or mind while feeling is in the heart. However, Mark and Jesus talk about perceiving in the spirit, and reasoning in the heart (v. 8).

6. The scribes' response to Jesus' statements and to the healing is not recorded (that is, no scribal response is singled out or distinguished from the general response of "all" the people recorded in v. 12), even though Jesus asks them two questions and the crowd's response to the healing is recorded (entire passage).

Possible Interpretations and Questions Based on These Observations

Obviously, the following interpretations are far from exhaustive. The first three interpretations tend to be negative because they are meant to show that interpretations must be based on the evidence from the text rather than on assumptions which are brought to the text, and that all varieties of interpretations must be considered before you come to a conclusion.

1. Based on observations 2 and 6. We cannot interpret this to mean that the paralytic did not speak, or that the scribes did not have a distinct response. Nor can we assume that the scribes are included in the "all" of verse 12. All we can say is that no speaking on the part of the paralytic, and no distinct response on the part of the scribes, is *recorded*. Both the paralytic and the scribes *may* have said much more than is recorded in this passage. Arguments and interpretations which are based on silence of the record are often very weak. (More is

said about the dangers of using arguments from silence in chapter 13.)

2. Based on observation 1. Again we need to be very careful lest we try to get too much out of this observation. For instance, we cannot conclude that the paralytic himself did not have faith, for he *may* be included in the word *their*. Also, we cannot conclude that Jesus did not address the men who brought the paralytic. To conclude thus would be another argument from silence.

3. Based on observations 2 and 3. It could easily be assumed that the paralytic was brought to Jesus so that he could be healed. But it is also *possible* that the paralytic was brought simply so that he could hear Jesus teach. Was this why Jesus responded to their faith by forgiving his sins? When all the information in the passage is put together with the information from the context of this passage and from the parallel accounts of this incident in Matthew and Luke, it appears quite *likely* that the paralytic was indeed brought so that he could be healed. The point is: don't assume anything. Don't take anything for granted. Give fair consideration to a wide variety of ways of putting the evidence together. All the different interpretations that come to your attention, from whatever source, should be tested against the evidence of the text.

4. Based on observation 4. Whereas it is debatable whether forgiving sins or healing is easier, *there is no question* that *saying* "your sins are forgiven" is easier than *saying* "arise, . . . walk." Telling someone his sins are forgiven is easy because it can be said without anyone being able to check. There is no visible evidence available for people to see whether you have authority in that realm and whether what was spoken has actually taken place. However, it is not easy to tell a paralyzed person to walk because everyone can readily see

whether or not you have authority in that realm by simply watching to see if the paralyzed person gets up and
walks. Even though Jesus had authority in both realms,
he knew that the scribes could not check up on him in the
realm of forgiving sins, which they had questioned. So
he showed them his authority in another supernatural
realm, healing, in which they could easily check his
authority. Having seen a demonstration of Jesus' authority in one supernatural realm, the scribes would
logically be forced to be open to the possibility of Jesus
having authority in the other.

It is especially important that you understand what an
observation is and how it differs from an interpretation,
because, in the actual Bible study procedures suggested
in chapters 17 and 18, observation and interpretation
are not differentiated for you. It is impossible to organize the actual steps of Bible study so that a certain set
of steps incorporates only observations, while the next
set of steps incorporates only interpretation. Rather,
varying degrees of both observation and interpretation
may at times enter into many of the steps. Since you cannot neatly separate them in your procedure, it is all the
more important that you be able to separate them in
your thinking. *You need to know during any step of the
procedure when you are observing and when you are interpreting so that you can truly make your observations
the basis of your interpretations.*

9

Pitfalls and
Perseverance in Observation

The first pitfall has to do with the tendency to miss the meaning that is expressly stated in a passage because you are busily looking for minute details and hidden clues to the meaning of the passage. Many passages will say exactly what they mean in language that is clear enough to be understood at the very first reading. *Do not overlook the clear, straightforward statements of the passage.*

The second pitfall has to do with the problem of a subjective or biased personal approach to the Bible. If you come to the Bible desiring to prove your side of the debate, or looking only for a particular set of evidence, you will probably "find" it there whether it is really there or not. If you are hoping to find some particular statement in the text, you will surely miss much of the rest of what the text has to say. If you already have a personal preference for a certain view, you will probably interpret some passages incorrectly so as to maintain your view. These approaches are a misuse of the Bible. Instead, we need to be as objective and detached as possible during the observation and interpretation phases of Bible study. In other words, personal desires and preferences must be set aside in order to ensure completeness and accuracy of observation and reasonableness of interpretation. Later, when the best interpretation is finally determined, and when that interpretation has practical implications for your life, *then* your approach should become quite personal as you submit your will and your life to the Word of God. But up to the point of application, objectivity is the only safe approach to take.

The third pitfall has to do with the temptation to get more out of the text than is actually there. Quite often a person feels he is not doing things right unless he comes up with striking (fresh, new) observations or profound (deep and far-reaching) interpretations. He may also be disappointed if he does not get a "blessing" every time he studies his Bible. If you aim for spectacular results you will always end up getting more out of the text than is actually there, which means that those additional ideas are coming from somewhere other than the biblical text. Your task is not to make something profound out of the text. Rather, your task is to find out exactly what the text says and means. There are enough profound ideas *in the text* so that, as you discover them, your Bible study will automatically be quite profound. You do not need to try to create profound interpretations. Instead, discover them. "Do not add to His words/ Lest He reprove you, and you be proved a liar" (Prov. 30:6).

Some people make the mistake of taking their clue to Bible study from the way many Bible experts teach or the way many pastors preach. However, Bible study should not follow the same pattern as teaching or preaching. It is fairly common for a speaker to speak in such a way that it appears that he is getting volumes out of one verse. He may begin by reading a verse and then discuss all the implications, ramifications, translations, transliterations, manifestations, interpretations, misinterpretations, applications, and misapplications of that single verse. The person who is listening to all of this may feel that the speaker was very observant indeed to get all of those thoughts out of the verse. But, of course, he didn't. Many of those thoughts came from the speaker's extensive background and training, and from his knowledge of the whole Bible and the whole field of theology, and from his years of experience. And, of course, it is good for the speaker to bring all of this to bear on his explanation of the text. But you must not try to adopt this pattern as your Bible study approach. Your task during the observation phase of Bible study is to get all the information which any given text has to yield—no more, and no less.

Perseverance

Making observations requires time and hard work. Keep looking. Never assume that you have seen all there is to see. Concentrate and keep looking. Then concentrate more and keep looking more. Then set it aside and come back later for some more concentrated searching. *Keep looking.* Sometimes observations will come to mind faster than you can write them down. Other times observations will come with painful slowness. Keep looking.

Over one hundred years ago Louis Agassiz, a well-known naturalist and Harvard professor, would encourage his students to persevere in the direct, inductive study of nature. Here is an example of how perseverance plus a few key practices in observation paid off for one of those students.

The Student, the Fish, and Agassiz

by the Student

(abridged)

It was more than fifteen years ago that I entered the laboratory of Professor Agassiz, and told him I had enrolled my name in the scientific school as a student of natural history. He asked me a few questions about my object in coming, my antecedents generally, the mode in which I afterwards proposed to use the knowledge I might acquire, and finally, whether I wished to study any special branch. To the latter I replied that while I wished to be well grounded in all departments of zoology, I purposed to devote myself specially to insects.

"When do you wish to begin?" he asked.

"Now," I replied.

This seemed to please him, and with an energetic "Very well," he reached from a shelf a huge jar of specimens in yellow alcohol.

"Take this fish," said he, "and look at it; we call it a Haemulon (pronounced Hem-yú-lon); by and by I will ask what you have seen."

With that he left me, but in a moment returned with explicit instructions as to the care of the object entrusted to me.

"No man is fit to be a naturalist," said he, "who does not know how to take care of specimens."

I was to keep the fish before me in a tin tray, and occasionally moisten the surface with alcohol from the jar, always taking care to replace the stopper tightly. . . . The example of the professor who had unhesitatingly plunged to the bottom of the jar to produce the fish was infectious; and though this alcohol had "a very ancient and fishlike smell," I really dared not show any aversion within these sacred precincts, and treated the alcohol as though it were pure water. . . .

In ten minutes I had seen all that could be seen in that fish, and started in search of the professor, who had, however, left the museum, and when I returned, after lingering over some of the odd animals stored in the upper apartment, my specimen was dry all over. I dashed the fluid over the fish as if to resuscitate it from a fainting-fit, and looked with anxiety for a return of the normal, sloppy appearance. This little excitement over, nothing was to be done but return to a steadfast gaze at my mute companion. Half an hour passed, an hour, another hour; the fish began to look loathsome. I turned it over and around; looked it in the face—ghastly; from behind, beneath, above, sideways, at a three-quarters' view—just as ghastly. I was in despair; at an early hour I concluded that lunch was necessary; so with infinite relief, the fish was carefully replaced in the jar, and for an hour I was free.

On my return, I learned that Professor Agassiz had been at the museum, but had gone and would not return for several hours. My fellow students were too busy to be disturbed by continued conversation. Slowly I drew forth that hideous fish, and with a feeling of desperation again looked at it. I might not use a magnifying glass; instruments of all kinds were interdicted. My two hands, my two eyes, and the fish; it seemed a most limited field. I pushed my fingers down its throat to see how sharp its teeth were. I began to count the scales in the different rows until I was convinced that that was nonsense. At last a happy thought struck me—I would draw the fish; and now with surprise I began to discover new features in the creature. Just then the professor returned.

"That is right," said he, "a pencil is one of the best eyes. I am glad to notice, too, that you keep your specimen wet and your bottle corked."

With these encouraging words he added,—

"Well, what is it like?"

He listened attentively to my brief rehearsal of the structure of parts whose names were still unknown to me: the fringed gill—arches and movable operculum; the pores of the head, fleshly lips, and lidless eyes; the lateral line, the spinous fin, and forked tail; the compressed and arched body. When I had finished, he waited as if expecting more, and then, with an air of disappointment:

"You have not looked very carefully; why," he continued, more earnestly, "you haven't seen one of the most conspicuous features of the animal, which is as plainly before your eyes as the fish itself. Look again; look again!" and he left me to my misery.

I was piqued; I was mortified. Still more of that wretched fish? But now I set myself to the task with a will, and discovered one new thing after another, until I saw how just the professor's criticism had been. The afternoon passed quickly, and then, towards its close, the professor inquired,

"Do you see it yet?"

"No," I replied, "I am certain I do not, but I see how little I saw before."

"That is next best," said he earnestly, "but I won't hear you now; put away your fish and go home; perhaps you will be ready with a better answer in the morning. I will examine you before you look at the fish."

This was disconcerting. Not only must I think of my fish all night, studying, without the object before me, what this unknown but most visible feature might be, but also, without reviewing my new discoveries, I must give an exact account of them the next day. I had a bad memory. . . .

The cordial greeting from the professor the next morning was reassuring. Here was a man who seemed to be quite as anxious as I that I should see for myself what he saw.

"Do you perhaps mean," I asked, "that the fish has symmetrical sides with paired organs?"

His thoroughly pleased, "Of course, of course!" repaid the wakeful hours of the previous night. After he had discoursed most happily and enthusiastically—as he always did—upon the importance of this point, I ventured to ask what I should do next.

"Oh, look at your fish!" he said, and left me again to my own devices. In a little more than an hour he returned and heard my new catalogue.

"That is good, that is good!" he repeated, "but that is not all; go on." And so, for three long days, he placed that fish before my eyes, forbidding me to look at anything else, or to use any artificial aid. "Look, look, look," was his repeated injunction.

This was the best . . . lesson I ever had—a lesson whose influence has extended to the details of every subsequent study; a legacy the professor has left to me, as he left it to many others, of inestimable value, which we could not buy, with which we cannot part. . . .

The fourth day a second fish of the same group was placed beside the first, and I was bidden to point out the resemblances and difference between the two; another and another followed, until the entire family lay before me, and a whole legion of jars covered the table and surrounding shelves; the odor had become a pleasant perfume. . . .

The whole group of Haemulons was thus brought into view; and whether engaged upon the dissection of the internal organs, preparation and examination of the bony framework, or the descriptions of the various parts, Agassiz's training in the method of observing facts and their orderly arrangement, was ever accompanied by the urgent exhortation not to be content with them.

"Facts are stupid things," he would say, "until brought into connection with some general law."

At the end of eight months, it was almost with reluctance that I left these friends and turned to insects; but what I gained by this outside experience has been of greater value than years of later investigation in my favorite groups.[1]

Note

1. *Appendix American Poems* (probably Boston: Houghton, Osgood and Co. 1880). From *Independent Bible Study* by Irving L. Jensen. Copyright 1963. Moody Press, Moody Bible Institute of Chicago. Used by permission.

10

Interpretation

The term *hermeneutics* refers to the set of principles or rules which govern one's interpretation of a piece of literature. The term *exegesis* refers to the actual practice of getting the meaning out of the text. Thus, hermeneutics is the theory; exegesis is the practice. Hermeneutics applied becomes exegesis. This chapter and the next two chapters very briefly discuss hermeneutics and exegesis.

As you recall from chapter 7, an observation differs from an interpretation, which differs from an application. An observation is a statement regarding something factual which is indicated directly in the text. An interpretation is based on observations and is a statement of the meaning of the text. However, an application is *not* a statement, either about what the text says, or about what it means, or about how it can be used to change one's life. Rather, an application is the use of the Bible (the Bible's teachings, principles, etc.) in one's life based on the proper interpretation.

Discovery in the Bible has much in common with discovery in other literature. However, response to the Bible has little in common with response to other literature. It is this second fact that causes some people to overgeneralize and claim that one's *entire* experience with the Bible (both discovery and response) must be

quite different than one's experience with all other literature. Thus, some claim that you should not try to study
the Bible in the same way you study other literature.
This claim is an oversimplification and is quite misleading.

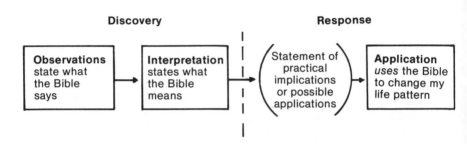

Consider the three main phases in the diagram above:
observation, interpretation, and application. In regard
to the first phase, observation of a passage from the
Bible is done nearly identically to observation of passages from other literature. Observation is the most
objective and concrete of the three phases. It involves
simply finding out what the text says, and this is done
practically the same way for both biblical and nonbiblical literature. This means that the skills, operations,
and practices used in observing a biblical text are very
similar to those used in the careful study of any piece of
literature.

However, in regard to the second phase, there is only
some similarity between interpretation of the Bible and
interpretation of other literature. This is true because
of two very unique facts about the Bible. First, the Bible

is inspired (2 Tim. 3:16*a*; 2 Pet. 1:21). In other words, the Bible is a completely reliable record which says exactly what God intended it to say. Everything that it records is recorded accurately, even the false statements of Satan and unbelievers. The Bible's complete reliability is one of its differences from all other literature. Thus, in interpreting the Bible, we must respect its content in a way we respect no other book. With other books we can often use our own experience, common sense, and logic to judge that a statement in a particular book is incorrect. But we can never act as a judge of the content of the Bible. Our interpretation of the Bible, although it will make full use of our minds, will never set our minds or our experience above the Bible. That is, as a person interprets a Bible passage, he cannot rightfully say, "I know what it says and I know what it means, but what it says and what it means are wrong."

Second, some of the Bible's teachings run counter to our own good opinion of ourselves. Thus, at times its message is unacceptable to us. Since we cannot welcome the Bible's message, we will tend very strongly to interpret (actually *mis*interpret) its message in such a way as to save our good opinion of ourselves. Such interpretation, of course, is extremely poor, since we are allowing the Bible to say only what we want it to say. Apart from the Holy Spirit we are unable to correctly understand the spiritual teachings in the Bible (1 Cor. 2:14). So, because the Bible is a spiritual and moral book, and we are by nature antispiritual and antimoral, we will tend to misinterpret many of the Bible's teachings. It is very important to note, however, that it is primarily one's *attitude* toward the Bible and its teachings (including one's assumptions about one's own nature) which causes the problems. When it comes to the skills, etc., used in interpreting the Bible, these remain basically the same as one would use with other literature.

In regard to the third phase, there is very little similarity between the application of the Bible and the application of other literature in our lives. Because of the Bible's complete reliability and its focus on spiritual and moral matters, and because of our own antispiritual and antimoral tendencies, we are under obligation to use the Bible to change our lives, as we are under obligation to no other book. (More is said about application in chapter 14.)

In a nutshell: we can expect that Bible study will use many of the same observational skills, hermeneutical rules, and exegetical practices as we would use in the interpretation of other literature. However, our attitudes toward the Bible (the respect we hold for it and the obedience we owe to it) are unique.

The remainder of this chapter and chapters 11 and 12 contain a very brief introduction to the general rules and principles of Bible interpretation. There is much excellent material written on this subject which you should read carefully. Several sources are recommended at the end of this chapter.

Many of the general principles discussed in these chapters are principles which you are already using on other writings, such as letters from your friends, novels, and textbooks. When it comes to Bible study, we do not throw out these principles which we use by common sense on other literature unless there is something different about the nature of the particular biblical passage which demands a different principle.

The Interpreter's Task

Many things that we read are relatively easy for us to interpret simply because we know the writer and the circumstances surrounding the writing, as when we receive a letter from a friend, or because we know the culture, as when we read an American newspaper. However, the Bible was written by men whom we have not known personally, in cultural settings and circumstances which we have not experienced, and in languages which are not our mother tongue. Thus, our most fundamental task in interpreting the Bible is to *comprehend the mind of the writer* and the original readers. This involves the writer's and original readers' language, their historical and cultural setting, their personal backgrounds, and the immediate circumstances, which along with the particular message (passage) being written all go together to comprise the mind of the writer and original readers. The interpreter's task is not to find *an* interpretation which fits the passage according to our times and ways of thinking. Rather, his task is to reach back and grasp the mind of the writer and original readers—*the* interpretation which fits the passage according to their times and ways of thinking.

Granted, according to 1 Peter 1:10-12, there are some prophetic passages which can be more clearly understood *after* a predicted event has taken place. But this fact does not mean that we should approach these or any other Bible passages from our own perspective rather than the writer's perspective. Even these prophetic passages must be seen first from the eyes of the writer. Even though the picture might be more complete or more concrete after the predicted event has occurred, that completed picture must start with the partial picture in the mind of the writer. Pieces which finish a puzzle are not even considered to be part of the same puzzle unless they fit what is already there. So we must know what is there first. We must see it as the writer saw it before we can properly fill in the final details. Furthermore, in such cases, it is this partial picture which comprises the complete mind of the writer and which is properly called the interpretation of the passage. The complete picture is better called the fulfillment, or actualization, or satisfaction of the passage.

The interpreter's task in all cases is to get back to the mind of the writer, to grasp *his* thought and intent within *his* time and setting.

Preference for the Original Languages

Since the books of the Bible were inspired in their original languages (mainly Hebrew and Greek), and since no translation can completely reproduce the thought, intent, idiom, and mood of the original, we prefer to study the Bible in the original languages. This is why the Bible scholar endeavors to master Hebrew and Greek.

While many peoples still do not have the Bible in their native language, we are very fortunate indeed to have many good translations of the Bible in English. But whenever possible we prefer to study the Greek New Testament and the Hebrew Old Testament. Of course, the ideal goal would be to fully master both Greek and Hebrew, but even a little knowledge of these languages can be helpful. For example, merely learning the names, appearances, sounds, and order of the letters in, say, the Greek alphabet has several advantages. First, by learning the names and appearances of the letters you will begin to break down the total unfamiliarity of Greek which mystifies many people. Second, by learning the sound of each letter you will be able to pronounce Greek words when you see them. This will help you remember Greek words that you find in a commentary or

Bible dictionary, and will help you recognize them when
you hear your pastor or a Bible teacher refer to them.
Third, by learning the order of the letters in the Greek
alphabet you will be able to find the definition(s) of any
Greek word in a Greek-English lexicon (dictionary). So,
even though you may think that you will never master
Greek or Hebrew, you should learn *something* about
these languages, and then continue to learn as much
about them as you can. You can find the Greek and Hebrew alphabets in many English dictionaries by looking
up the word *alphabet,* and in the back of *Strong's Exhaustive Concordance.* For further study of Greek see J.
Gresham Machen's *New Testament Greek for Begin-
ners* or Ray Summers' *Essentials of New Testament
Greek.* For further study of Hebrew see Kyle M. Yates'
The Essentials of Biblical Hebrew, revised edition,
edited by John J. Owens, Thomas O. Lambdin's *An Introduction to Biblical Hebrew,* or Menahem Mansoor's *Biblical Hebrew Step by Step.*

A caution is necessary, however, in connection with
the use of Greek and Hebrew. A little knowledge of one
or both of these languages *can* be a dangerous thing, if it
is thought that that knowledge is *the* key to correct
Bible interpretation, or it is thought that that knowledge *replaces* other rules of interpretation. Even the
full mastery of Greek and Hebrew does not replace all
the other rules of interpretation and the principles and
procedures of proper Bible study. For instance, the person who knows Greek but neglects the other principles
is on very flimsy ground. He can make many of the very
same mistakes that lead to incorrect interpretations in
the Greek that he can make in English. Knowledge of
Greek is no guarantee of proper interpretation of New
Testament passages. Nearly all of the principles explained in this guidebook must be used in a study of the

Bible in the original languages, just as they must be used in a study of the Bible in an English translation. A person who prayerfully and carefully follows proper interpretation principles and study procedures as he studies a good English translation will nearly always arrive at a better interpretation of a given passage than the person who studies the Greek text but ignores proper principles and procedures. This means that a person should work hard to learn and apply the correct Bible study approach whether or not he knows the original languages. Of course, everything else being equal, knowledge of Greek and Hebrew *is* a decided asset in Bible study. What is preferred is to have *both* a good knowledge of Greek and Hebrew *and* to use all the other principles as you study the Bible in the original languages. (More is said about English translations and their use in chapter 16.)

Singularity of Interpretation

Messages can be written in either a direct or an indirect manner. On the one hand, if we want someone to be sure to get the point, we will try to write out our idea in clear, explicit language that is directly on the subject. On the other hand, we might merely imply the idea indirectly, but then we run the risk of having the reader miss the point altogether. Furthermore, even our explicit statements may convey ideas which we do not consciously intend to express.

All of this points up how dangerous it would be for an interpreter to focus his attention on implicit or unconscious meanings. It is best to assume that the biblical writers wanted their readers to get the point and to focus their attention on explicit statements. Our task, then, as interpreters is to find that single, central message. Of course, the exploration of several possible meanings for a given passage will often be part of the discovery process, but our goal is to find *the* meaning. Even when we detect additional significance implied in the passage, as illustrated on page 62, that additional interpretation must not be allowed to replace or overshadow the single, explicit teaching of the passage.

Every Bible passage has a single meaning, only one correct interpretation of its central idea, even though that one interpretation might have many different applications. After we have discovered *the* correct interpretation of a passage, we can apply that interpretation to as many practical situations as we like, but the interpretation of the passage remains singular.

Recording Interpretations

Once you have interpreted a passage or something within a passage, how should you record your interpretation? There is an important difference between the way observations are recorded and the way interpretations are recorded. As illustrated in chapter 8 ("Observations on Mark 2:1-12"), observations are stated with complete certainty because they are directly verifiable in the text. In other words, after one person states an observation, anyone else should also be able to go to the text and say, "Yes, that is exactly what the text says." Interpretations, however, have varying degrees of certainty. Interpretations should be stated so as to express the actual degree of certainty present, that is, how firmly this interpretation is based on observations, and how likely it is that this interpretation is better than all other interpretations. As you state each interpretation, you should use phrases like the ones in the chart below in order to express your degree of certainty—anywhere from complete certainty to complete uncertainty.

Most certain   Surely . . . / Certainly . . . / Without question . . .
                Probably . . . / It is very likely that . . .
                Evidently . . . / It seems that . . .
                Perhaps . . . / Maybe . . . / It is possible that . . .
Least certain   Is . . .? / Did . . .? / Were . . .? / Why . . .?

If you look back at the interpretations given in chapter 8 you will see that the degree of certainty is stated in each interpretation.

Patience

Both observation and interpretation, if done properly, require much time and hard work. If you want to have confidence in your interpretations, there are no short-cuts.

Do not be afraid of raising a lot of questions which you are not able to answer easily. Having unanswered questions is not a sign of ignorance. Rather, it is a sign of ignorance when a person announces that he knows everything about a certain Bible passage or topic. Many people are not aware of just how much they do not know. But becoming aware of an unanswered question is the first step toward answering that question. Thus, you should ask all the questions you can, and do not be discouraged if, early in the process, you have many more questions than answers.

In fact, leaving a question unanswered *until* you are ready to answer it is an ability you should develop. Many people, feeling uncomfortable with unanswered questions, jump to an answer mainly for the security of having an answer. However, you must suspend judgment until all the facts are in, and until you have considered many possible answers. This requires patience and diligence. "He who gives an answer before he hears, It is folly and shame to him" (Prov. 18:13). It is better to crawl carefully to a conclusion and be correct than to leap blindly and be incorrect. Two questions which you should continually ask yourself during Bible study are:

1. Do I have all the relevant facts?
2. Have I considered a wide variety of interpretations?

Keep in mind that the basic and essential truths in the Bible are clear and straightforward. You do not have to dig and dig and weigh and weigh for years to discover the basic biblical teachings about whether or not man is a sinner, whether or not Jesus died for our sins, whether or not a positive relationship with God will be reestablished if we trust in Jesus Christ, etc. These and other basics are clearly and convincingly taught in the Bible. If these basics are doubted, it is not because the Bible is not clear on these topics; it is because people have come to the Bible with unfounded assumptions and closed minds and thus have clouded the abundant and explicit evidence in the Bible on these matters. Thus, we do not need to fear that we will be left without the basic answers that we need for our spiritual life and growth. However, we do need to be ready to suspend our judgment on some secondary issues. A number of passages in the New Testament (Matt. 23:23; Heb. 5:12 to 6:1; Luke 10:40-42; 2 Pet. 3:16; 1 Cor. 3:2) indicate that there are some matters in the Bible which are more weighty, more elementary, more necessary, and more clear than other matters. Thus, the careful Bible student will distinguish between what is primary and what is secondary. He will work for the best answers on even the secondary issues, but he will also show humility and love toward others and tolerance toward their views on the secondary matters when they differ from his.

For Further Reading

The brief introduction to general hermeneutics found in this chapter and the next two chapters should be supplemented with further reading in this important field. If you are serious about Bible study you will want to read as much as you can about these principles of interpretation. Any time spent in reading the sources listed below will be well worth the effort. (The first few sources in the list are the shortest and easiest ones.)

Furthermore, you will often be confronted with specialized types of literature such as poetry, prophecy, parables, and apocalyptic writings. There are specialized hermeneutical rules which apply to the interpretation of each of these special types of literature. It is beyond the scope of this guidebook to explain all of these special hermeneutical rules. However, most of the sources listed below have long sections devoted to special hermeneutics which deserve your thoughtful consideration.

Dickason, Fred. "Straight Thinking in Bible Interpretation," *Moody Monthly,* February 1964, pp. 22-23, 60-65.

Stibbs, Alan M. *Understanding God's Word.* Downers Grove, Illinois: Inter-Varsity Press, 1950.

Sterrett, T. Norton. *How to Understand Your Bible,* rev. ed. Downers Grove, Illinois: Inter-Varsity Press, 1974 (especially sections II and III).

Mickelsen and Mickelsen. *Better Bible Study.* Glendale, California: Regal Books, 1977.

Pentecost, J. Dwight. *Things to Come: A Study in Biblical Eschatology.* Grand Rapids, Michigan: Dunham Pub. Co., 1958, chapters 1-4.

Berkhof, Louis. *The Principles of Biblical Interpretation.* Grand Rapids, Michigan: Baker Book House, 1950.

Ramm, Bernard. *Protestant Biblical Interpretation: A Textbook of Hermeneutics,* 3rd rev. ed. Grand Rapids, Michigan: Baker Book House, 1975.

Ramm, Bernard, and others. *Hermeneutics.* Grand Rapids, Michigan: Baker Book House, 1971.

Mickelsen, A. Berkeley. *Interpreting the Bible.* Grand Rapids, Michigan: Wm. B. Eerdmans, 1963.

Terry, Milton S. *Biblical Hermeneutics.* Grand Rapids, Michigan: Zondervan, n.d.

11

Literary Interpretation

Literary interpretation includes both literal and figurative interpretation.

The Bible *is* literature. Indeed it is a special class of literature, but it is still literature. Thus, our interpretation of the Bible must be literary, as it would be with other literature. The term "literary" is used to indicate that *our interpretation of the words and sentences in the Bible must be according to their literal and grammatical sense with proper place given to figurative elements in the text.*

Some statements in the Bible are to be interpreted literally. Some are to be interpreted figuratively. It is dangerous to interpret figuratively what should be interpreted literally. It is just as dangerous to interpret literally what should be interpreted figuratively. In the vast majority of cases the text does not explicitly tell that reader which type of interpretation should be used, although there are some cases in which Jesus' figurative statements are interpreted for us (John 2:19-21; 7:38-39). The literal interpretation of figurative statements caused confusion in Jesus' day (John 2:19-21; 6:51-52), and it will do the same for you. Thus, one of the interpreter's basic responsibilities is to sort out the literal statements and the figurative statements in the Bible. Always *begin* by understanding each word in its literal, normal, natural, straightforward, ordinary, plain sense according to the grammatical structure of the sentence, and *then* make whatever adjustments are called for by the figurative elements in the passage and the underlying *intent* of the writer. Make such adjustments *only* when they are called for by the text itself, which occurs when the figurative interpretation makes better sense in the immediate context than the literal interpretation. Only by (1) starting with the literal, and then (2) making the adjustments called for by the figurative, can you arrive at the correct interpretation of the Bible.

What is called *literary* interpretation here is often referred to as *literal* interpretation by others. But the term *literal* is misunderstood and misused if it is employed to describe one's interpretation of every word and sentence in the Bible. Those who say you should consistently follow a literal approach are *not* saying that you must interpret everything in the Bible literally. For example, a person may say that he understands the "thousand years" of Revelation 20:1-7 to mean one thousand actual years. Furthermore, he claims that he believes in a literal one thousand years *because* he believes in using literal interpretation consistently throughout the Bible. However, he certainly should not believe that Satan is a literal "dragon" or "serpent," or that Satan will be imprisoned in a literal "abyss" by a literal "key" and "chain," as though such physical objects could imprison a nonphysical spirit. Thus, even the person who claims to use a consistent literal approach to the Bible must incorporate *both* literal and figurative interpretation, often within the same passage. It is an oversimplification to think of one's approach to the Bible as *either* literal or nonliteral. In actuality, *our approach must start with the literal but then include both the literal and the figurative whenever the figurative is called for by the immediate context.* Remember, however, that you should always *begin* with a literal approach and retain that understanding of the passage unless there is good reason in the passage or its context to employ a figurative understanding.

Figures of speech vary in their degree of literalness. At one extreme there are figures such as litotes, simile, and parable whose meanings are nearly identical to their literal interpretations. At the other extreme there are figures such as hypothetical conjecture and irony whose meanings are contrary to their literal interpretations. Some of the common figures of speech are defined and illustrated in the following material. (Italics in the Scripture quotes were added by the author.)

1. **Litotes:** an understatement in which a point is made by stating the negative of the opposite point ("It *won't* be *long* now"; "That's *not* a *bad* idea").
John 6:37—"The one who comes to Me I will certainly *not cast out.*"
Galatians 5:23—"*Against* such things there is *no law.*"
1 Thessalonians 2:14-15—"The Jews, . . . killed the Lord Jesus. . . . They are *not pleasing to God.*"

2. **Simile:** an explicit comparison of two dissimilar things using "like" or "as" ("He sleeps *like a log*"; "cheeks *like roses*").
Isaiah 53:6—"All of us *like sheep* have gone astray."
Psalm 1:3—"He will be *like a tree.*"
1 Peter 5:8—"The devil, prowls about *like a roaring lion.*"
Matthew 25:32—"He will separate them from one another, *as the shepherd separates the sheep from the goats.*"

3. **Parable:** an extended simile; a story about everyday things that illustrates a single truth or principle.

See Matthew 13:24 and following verses.

4. **Metaphor:** an implied comparison in which one thing is spoken of as if it were another ("Mr. Smith is a *pillar* in the church"; "Bill *dived into* his studies").

Psalm 119:105—"Thy word is *a lamp to my feet.*"

2 Corinthians 5:4—"While we are in this *tent.*"

1 Corinthians 13:1—"I have become a *noisy gong.*"

Philippians 3:2—"Beware of the *dogs.*"

Luke 13:32—"Go and tell that *fox.*"

John 6:35—"I am the *bread* of life; he who *comes to* Me shall not *hunger*, and he who believes in Me shall never *thirst.*"

Psalm 18:2—"The Lord is my *rock.*"

1 Thessalonians 5:19—"Do not *quench* the Spirit."

5. **Allegory:** an extended metaphor; a story or fable about symbolic and often fictional characters or events that expresses a more complex truth or principle. See Daniel 2:31-45; John 10:1-16.

6. **Personification:** a type of metaphor; speaking about something as if it were a person ("duty *commands*"; "the *long arm* of the law").

Numbers 16:32—"The earth *opened its mouth and swallowed them up.*"

Proverbs 9:1-3—"Wisdom has *built her house.*"

Psalm 98:8—"Let the rivers *clap their hands*; Let the mountains *sing.*"

7. **Apostrophe:** addressing something as if it were a person, or addressing an absent or dead person as if he were present or alive ("*O Liberty*, what things are done in thy name!").

1 Kings 13:2—"*O altar, altar.*"

2 Samuel 18:33—"*O my son Absalom.*"

8. **Anthropomorphism:** a type of metaphor; speaking about God in terms of human characteristics.

Deuteronomy 11:2—"The Lord . . . His *mighty hand,* and His *outstretched arm.*"

9. **Euphemism:** an understatement using a mild or more agreeable expression instead of a blunt expression of an unpleasant or offensive idea ("the *departed*" referring to the dead).

Genesis 4:1—"Now the man *knew* his wife; and she conceived" (marginal reading).

1 Corinthians 15:6—"Most of whom remain until now, but some have *fallen asleep.*"

10. **Hyperbole:** deliberate extreme overstatement and excessive exaggeration ("She is *centuries* old").

Deuteronomy 1:28—"The cities are large and fortified *to heaven.*"

11. **Synecdoche:** substitution of a part for the whole or vice versa, an individual for a class or vice versa, singular for plural or vice versa, genus for species or vice versa, abstract for concrete or vice versa, absolute for relative or vice versa, or the material components for the thing made of them, etc. ("The Millers live *three doors* up the street from us"; "the *creature,*" referring to man).

2 Samuel 16:21—"The *hands* . . . will . . . be strengthened."

Galatians 1:16—"Consult with *flesh and blood.*"

Psalm 51:4—"Against Thee, *Thee only,* I have sinned."

12. **Metonymy:** the substitution of an associated term for the name itself ("The *White House* announced today"; "The *kettle* is boiling").

Psalm 23:5—"Thou dost prepare a *table* before me."

Matthew 3:5—"*Jerusalem* was going out to him."

Matthew 18:16—"By the *mouth* of two or three witnesses."

13. **Symbol:** something that, besides standing for it-

self, stands for something else because of relationship or convention, especially the repeated use of a visible sign of something invisible or a natural sign of something supernatural (for example, the *oak* as a symbol of strength).

See Genesis 9:13 and Matthew 26:26-28 where the establishment of the *rainbow* and the *bread* and *cup* as symbols is discussed.

Matthew 27:51—"The *veil* of the temple was torn in two."

Hebrews 9:14—"How much more will the *blood* of Christ, . . . cleanse your conscience."

Isaiah 1:18—"Though your sins are as *scarlet,*/They will be as *white* as snow."

See Acts 10:9-16,34-35.

(Beware of thinking that every symbol has a consistent meaning throughout the Bible. For instance, compare the "serpent" in John 3:14 and Rev. 20:2, and the "lion" in Rev. 5:5 and 1 Pet. 5:8. Also, the "little horn" of Dan. 7:8, which is part of the fourth empire, is not the same king as the one represented by the "rather small horn" of Dan. 8:9, which is part of the third empire.)

14. **Exclamatory rhetorical question** (or interrogation): a point is made by asking, but not answering, a question with an obvious or implied answer.

Isaiah 40:13—"Who has directed the Spirit of the Lord,/ Or as His counselor has informed Him?"

Romans 8:35—"Who shall separate us from the love of Christ?"

James 3:11—"Does a fountain send out from the same opening both fresh and bitter water?"

15. **Hypothetical conjecture:** a fictional or impossible case cited for the purpose of portraying the logical outcomes of a false premise and not meant to describe an actual situation.

1 Corinthians 15:29—"What will those do who are baptized for the dead? If the dead are not raised at all, why then are they baptized for them?"
(Matt. 5:29-30 *may* also be understood to be a hypothetical conjecture in light of Matt. 5:20; 15:19; 23:25-28.)
    16. **Irony:** an expression which means the opposite of its literal interpretation, sometimes sarcastic.
Job 12:2—"With you wisdom will die."

These, and other types of figures of speech demonstrate the abundance and variety of figurative material in the Bible, as in all of human language. Figurative elements are especially common in such literary molds as poetic, apocalyptic, and parabolic passages. Knowing the technical name for each type of figure is not as important as being able to discern the developing thought and the intent of the writer in any given passage. It is the *meaning* of a figure of speech, not the figure's technical label, which should be your main concern.

As you attempt to interpret a figure of speech which you find in the Bible, remember that the two primary determinants of the meaning of the figure are (1) the literal interpretation of the figure, and (2) the immediate context surrounding the figure. In all figures of speech, the real meaning of the figure is related in some way to (determined in the light of) the literal interpretation of the figure. Always begin with the figure's literal interpretation. With the exception of litotes, simile, and parable, the literal interpretation of the figure gives a more or less distorted meaning in the sense that the literal interpretation does not fully harmonize with the immediate context. This, of course, is what helps you identify the fact that you are dealing with a figure of speech in the first place. In many cases, a knowledge of the various types of figures of speech will then help you move from the literal interpretation of the figure to the real meaning of the figure. When you feel that you have arrived at the true meaning of the figure of speech, write out a literal statement of that exact same idea without using any figurative expressions at all. Then substitute your literal restatement in place of the figure in the text to see if the context is satisfied by your literal restatement.

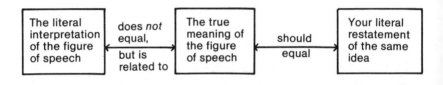

For example, a metaphor:

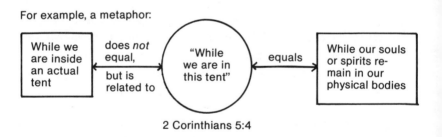

2 Corinthians 5:4

For example, an anthropomorphism:

Deuteronomy 11:2

For example, a euphemism:

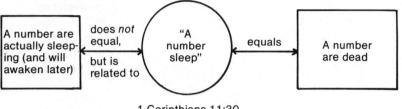

1 Corinthians 11:30

Some people deny much of the figurative element in the Bible because they have a misunderstanding about figurative language. They mistakenly equate the literal with the material or physical and the figurative with the spiritual. However, such an equation is invalid since something that is material can be described figuratively (for example, "the cities are large and fortified to heaven," Deut. 1:28), and something that is spiritual can be stated literally (for example, "God is spirit"). Likewise, they might equate the literal with the true, the factual, and the historical, and the figurative with the mystical, the ethereal, the unhistorical (or suprahistorical). Again, such an equation is invalid, since that which is true can just as easily be spoken of in either literal or figurative terms. When you interpret a passage figuratively you are not necessarily saying that what it describes is not actually true or concrete.

Also, some people deny much of the figurative element in the Bible because they mistakenly equate figurative interpretation with extreme allegorical interpretation. In literary interpretation, whether a specific element in the text is being interpreted literally or figuratively, the meaning is derived *from* the text. However, in extreme allegorical interpretation (which is not the same as interpreting an allegory) *meaning is arbitrarily*

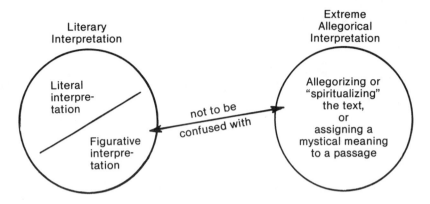

added to the text, and this added meaning is considered to be the real or preferred meaning of the passage. For example, one might arbitrarily interpret "heaven" to mean the mind, "sea" to mean the present age, or the "four rivers" of Genesis 2:10 to mean the four virtues of prudence, temperance, courage, and justice. Such allegorizing is deductive rather than inductive. While it is true that extreme allegorical interpretation is invalid and should be avoided, it does not follow that figurative interpretation is invalid or should be avoided. In other words, even though extreme allegorical interpretation should be given no place at all, figurative interpretation should still be given its proper place as part of literary interpretation.

12

Contextual Interpretation

The meanings of words, phrases, and sentences are determined by their context.

The Biblical Context

Open up any dictionary and glance through the definitions of several common words. You will find that the words which we use most commonly nearly always have several different definitions. Yet, when you read one of those words in a letter or a novel you have little trouble deciding which definition is intended by the writer. This is possible because a word is ultimately defined not by its dictionary definition, or by its etymology, but it is defined by the way it is used in a particular context. The word *light* can be used in one context to refer to one thing and in a different context to refer to something else. The same is true for the word *pan* and the word *foot* and for most other common words. In each case it is the context which narrows down the meaning of the word. And, of course, context is just as important in determining the meaning of words in the Bible.

The same principle operates with phrases and sentences. If you have ever been quoted out of context, you can appreciate how this works. Another person may quote your entire sentence perfectly, but his understanding of what you meant is quite different from yours. So, you explain the context of your remark in order to help him understand the real meaning of that one sentence.

Here are two sentences which are quite ambiguous until we know what context surrounds them. "This house is empty." This sentence would mean something quite different when spoken by a furniture mover than when spoken by a person doing door-to-door visitation, and it would mean something different still when spoken by a widow. "There is no God" is part of a statement denying God's existence in many contexts, but it is part of a statement affirming God's existence in Psalm 53:1 and 1 Corinthians 8:4.

Thus, the meanings of words, phrases, and sentences are ultimately determined by their context. This fact about the relationship between context and the meaning of individual words, phrases, and sentences points to a procedure which can often help you find the best interpretation of an ambiguous phrase. Suppose you have a phrase which is vague or ambiguous; that is, the phrase could easily refer to two or more things. The problem is that, as you read the sentence substituting one possible meaning for the phrase, the sentence makes just as good sense as when you substitute any of the other possible meanings. However, this ambiguity can often be resolved by reading the entire paragraph, making the same substitutions just mentioned. Often the addition of more context will help you discern which of the several possible meanings best fits the whole movement of thought in the passage.

Context is vitally important in interpretation. You need to make a conscious effort always to look in the context for important information that will help you inter-

pret a word, phrase, or sentence. The context may help
you find out such things as:

1. Who is speaking here?
2. To whom is he speaking?
3. To what and whom do these pronouns refer?
4. How does the writer introduce this section? How
   does this section relate to the ones immediately
   before and after it? Has the writer stated what the
   purpose of this passage is (to illustrate a point
   made earlier, to answer a question, etc.)? Is the
   point made in this passage illustrated later?
5. Is this word defined or used clearly in a nearby
   passage? Are there any qualifying phrases nearby
   that would affect the meaning?
6. What incident has just happened to bring on these
   comments?
7. What else has the writer said about this same subject elsewhere in this book?
8. When and where did this take place?

Often the answers to these and similar questions help
determine the correct interpretation of the passage.

Every word and phrase in the Bible must be interpreted in the context of its sentence, and each sentence
in the context of its paragraph. It is this *immediate* context which often contributes the most to the understanding of a word, phrase, or sentence. (The immediate context is usually considered to be the sentences which
come immediately before and immediately after the sentence under consideration.) But there are also larger
contexts which must be kept in mind. Each paragraph
must be interpreted in the context of its chapter, each
chapter in the context of its book, and each book in the
context of the Bible as a whole.

In the following two examples the context is indis-

pensable in determining the meaning of the passage.
First, consider Romans 3:23 in which Paul states that
"all have sinned." Many people think that this is one of
the several verses that prove that sin is universal, that
every human being, with the single exception of Jesus,
has sinned. However, the context does not allow such an
interpretation. Read the immediate context in verses
19-30. If, as some claim, verse 23 teaches that all humans have sinned, then verse 24 must teach that all
humans are justified, since both verses are describing
the same group of people. Actually, the word *all* in verse
23 refers to "all those who believe" mentioned in verse
22. Neither Jewish believers (who had the circumcision
and the Law) nor Gentile believers (who did not have the
circumcision or the Law) earned righteousness through
the Law. Verses 21-24 teach that, since both groups *of
believers* (Jewish believers and Gentile believers) were
sinners, there is no difference in the way they got their
righteousness. "All" (both groups) had to be justified,
not through the Law, but through faith in Jesus Christ.
Of course, it is true that all humans have sinned, as is
taught in verses 9-18, and this is why it is also true that
all those who believe have to obtain their righteousness
through faith rather than through works. But this does
not change the fact that verse 23 is talking about all believers, not all humans. Context is indispensable.

As a second example consider Luke 17:5 where Luke
records that the apostles once said to Jesus, "Increase
our faith!" No doubt, many have understood this to be a
noble request. But if you carefully examine the immediate context you will see that this request of the apostles
was far from noble. In fact, it was sharply rebuked by
Jesus. Note the immediate context in verses 3-10. Jesus
had just given the apostles a command. He told them
that they should repeatedly forgive a repentant brother

(v. 3-4). It was in response to this difficult command that
the apostles asked Jesus to increase their faith. Jesus
then demonstrated that, in connection with this particular command, the apostles had no faith to begin with, for
if they had had even the smallest amount of faith they
would have been able to relocate a tree at command (v. 6).
In other words, if the smallest amount of faith could
enable them to perform such a spectacular miracle, then
their admission of a lack of faith to carry out Jesus' command was in reality an admission of no faith at all in
regard to that particular command. The apostles' request for more faith implied that they had some already,
when they really did not. It also implied that, even after
they had received a command from Jesus, the responsibility was still on Jesus, not on them. Jesus clears up
this second misconception by reminding them of one of
the most basic facts in their culture, namely, that a slave
is expected to obey his master (vv. 7-9). Then Jesus
clearly states the implication of this fact for the apostles: the apostles should see themselves as slaves of the
Lord Jesus and should obey him (v. 10). Thus, Jesus'
command (in the context immediately before the apostles' request) and Jesus' response (in the context immediately after their request) make it clear that their
request was not good. A far better response to Jesus'
command would have been "Lord, we are your slaves,
and we will do what you have told us to do." Context is
indispensable.

As you study the whole Bible you become aware of the
fact that God's revelation of himself and of his will for
man has taken place gradually. As time progressed,
revelation became more and more complete. Of course,
God's basic approach to man has never changed. God has
always dealt with man in love and grace and has always
expected man to respond by trusting (having faith in)

him and obeying him. However, God's specific arrangements with man (precisely what God revealed to man including exactly what he expected man to do) varied from time to time throughout Bible history. These specific arrangements, or dispensations, must be kept in mind when interpreting passages from dispensations which differ from our own. For example, we must remember that the Old Testament saints did not have the full light of the life and teachings of Jesus Christ or the writings of the apostles, so we must understand these Old Testament saints' experiences and their statements in the context of the dispensation in which they lived. We cannot view those who lived under the old arrangement (the Law of Moses) as though they had the full revelation of the new arrangement (the new covenant, or the church age). Nor can we view those who lived before the Law as though they had the full revelation of the Law, much less that of the new arrangement. Every passage must be interpreted in the context of its own dispensation. There are important differences between the specific arrangements (dispensations) which must be remembered. But, of course, there are also similarities between the dispensations which must also be remembered. These similarities account for the fact that Abraham, who lived before the Law, can serve as an example of faith to us who live under the full revelation of the new arrangement (Heb. 11:8-12).

A great deal of emphasis must be placed on this principle of interpreting in light of the context, for this principle is violated very frequently. Although a person could plead ignorance in regard to some of the other tools or principles of interpretation (for instance, "I don't know Greek," or "I wasn't aware of that fact about the Babylonians"), he can never plead ignorance with this principle of interpreting in light of the context. The immediate context is readily available to all readers. To ignore the context is not really to read at all!

The Historical and Cultural Context

Most of our communication takes place within our own time-bound culture. Thus, we have little reason to think about how much our own time and culture influence our thought patterns and our communication. However, when we try to communicate with someone from a background which is vastly different from our own, we quickly feel the necessity of being able to see things from that person's world of thought. The communications of the Bible writers are much the same. It is true that the books of the Bible are inspired and are thus completely reliable. But it is also true that they were written so as to communicate most effectively to their primary audience, their original readers. This required that each book be written within the time and culture of the original readers, not in some suprahistorical or supracultural manner. Thus, our understanding of any Bible passage will be most accurate when it is the same understanding that the writer and the original readers had in their own time and culture. For instance, what were the prevalent thought patterns, attitudes toward authorities, historical occurrences, modes of travel, interpersonal manners and customs? The more we know about their historical setting and how they thought and lived, the closer we can come to the mind of the writer and the original readers in attempting to interpret a given Bible passage.

Only rarely does the Bible directly explain a custom (such as in Ruth 4:7 and John 4:9), because in the vast majority of cases the original readers were already quite familiar with the customs. Usually we must learn about the customs indirectly, from inferences about it in the passage or from something like a Bible commentary or Bible dictionary which gives information about these particular people and their practices taken from historical and archaeological sources. Knowledge of the customs can help you understand biblical events. For example, the Gospels refer to Jesus and others *reclining* at table (Matt. 26:7; etc.). It was customary then, when eating a meal, to remove one's sandals and recline on a couch or mat, resting on one elbow with the head toward the table. Such knowledge makes it much easier to visualize many of the events which occurred around meal scenes in the life of Jesus.

Also, each culture has its own unique linguistic expressions, called idioms. For instance, we would say that one sabbath comes "seven days" after the previous sabbath. But the apostle John expresses the same meaning by saying "eight days" after. This idiomatic expression grows out of their cultural practice of counting the first sabbath as day one, so that the following sabbath is day eight (similar to the way in which we label an octave in music). Compare, for instance, John 20:26 in the *New American Standard Bible* and the *New International Version*. Also, the Jews reckoned the time of day differently than we do, counting their hours from the beginning of the light period rather than from the middle. Again, compare Acts 2:15 in the *New American Standard Bible* and the *New International Version*. If the words in the idiom are translated into English in a literal word-for-word fashion rather than being translated idiomatically (the entire idiom in the original language being replaced by a phrase with the same meaning), you must be careful lest you interpret the phrase in a literal word-for-word fashion and arrive at a meaning quite different from the meaning of the idiom in the original language. Other idiomatic expressions can be discovered by studying the cultures and languages of the Old Testament and New Testament peoples.

Beware of Etymologies

Some people misunderstand the place of a word's etymology in determining the meaning of the word. Etymology involves the tracing of the various meanings which have been attached to a word in its past usage. Or, said another way, a word's etymology is the history of the way people have used that word. Some people believe that if you can find the etymology of a word in a commentary or a book of word studies, that etymology will give you the best clue to the word's meaning in any given passage. However, the following two principles support the conclusion that etymology should not be relied upon as *the* key to the interpretation of words. First, a word's *current* usage (the commonly accepted literal understanding of the word *at the time of writing*) should be your starting point in interpreting its meaning in any given context. Notice that it is the word's current usage, not its past usage, which is the starting point for interpreting the word. Second, words are ultimately defined by their context, as explained earlier in this chapter. Thus, even though etymologies are often interesting and they often help you appreciate a word's current usage, the word's etymology should never be made the primary determinant of the word's meaning. Instead, (1) the word's current usage and (2) the context in which the word is used are far more important in determining the meaning of that word. (More is said about word studies in chapter 18.)

Comparing Passage with Passage

Since the entire Bible was inspired by God, there are
no contradictions in it. When you compare one passage
with another, whether or not the passages are in the
same book and whether or not the passages are in the
same testament, they will harmonize with each other.
Of course, one of the passages may emphasize a different aspect of the truth, or may give a more complete picture of the truth, or may reflect the specific arrangements unique to a particular dispensation, but any such
differences are complementary to each other rather
than contradictory. Thus, if you are to arrive at a complete and balanced picture of the truth, you must compare passage with passage. This is especially so in
studying some of the narrative passages when the
events are recorded in two or more places in the Bible.
Many of the reminders and commands of Moses which
are recorded in the Book of Deuteronomy relate to
events and commands recorded in Exodus, Leviticus,
and Numbers. Many events recorded in 2 Samuel and 1
and 2 Kings are also recorded in 1 and 2 Chronicles. The
writings of the Prophets (in the Books of Isaiah through
Malachi) have their backgrounds in some of the historical books (1 Kings through Nehemiah). Many events in
the life of Jesus are recorded in more than one of the four
Gospels. And the writings of Paul (in Romans through
Philemon) have their backgrounds in the Book of Acts. It
is the responsibility of the Bible student when studying
one passage to seek out such related passages for comparison.

When doing topical study, it is also very important to
seek out different passages on the same topic for comparison. Finding such passages for comparison is made
much easier when a person has a good general knowl-

edge of the content of the Bible, but even the beginner will gain much help in finding different passages on the same subject from a concordance. (The steps for finding and using such related passages are described in chapter 18.)

For example, some people maintain that preachers, teachers, and counselors can have certainty that if they simply proclaim the Word of God, the Word will always greatly profit those who hear it. This viewpoint might be based on such passages as Isaiah 55:11 and Hebrews 4:12. However, these passages *by themselves* are not a sufficient basis for building your conclusions regarding when and how the Word will function. There are other passages which must be compared with these two passages. Elsewhere the Bible teaches that personal factors within the hearers affect when and how the Word functions, and sometimes the Word does not profit the hearers (John 16:12; Matt. 13:19-23; Heb. 4:2)! The study of a Bible topic is complete only when you have examined *all* that the Bible says on that topic. It is very dangerous to build a doctrine on one or two isolated verses.

A similar danger is the use of the false "first-mention" principle. Some people hold that the meaning of a word or the significance of an object is determined by the meaning or significance it has when it is first mentioned in the Bible. This idea, however, is a misleading oversimplification. Instead, examine *all* that the Bible says about it, not merely one other reference to it.

Whenever two passages *appear* to contradict each other, you must reexamine your interpretation of both passages. As a general rule you will find that one of the passages is less clear than the other. Perhaps it is a vague passage (ambiguous; easily capable of two or more interpretations). Perhaps it is an inferential passage (instead of speaking directly about the topic under consideration, it indirectly implies something about the topic). Less clear passages, that is, vague and inferential passages, must always be interpreted in the light of the clearer passages on that topic. This is a rule which is automatically used in everyday conversation and reading. By applying this rule to the study of the Bible many apparent contradictions can be easily resolved.

There will be instances, however, when the passages which appear to contradict each other will both seem to be quite clear. Remember that it can only be an apparent clarity and an apparent contradiction, since it is not possible for two true statements to be mutually exclusive. Further reexamination of both passages is called for. As you reexamine the passages, make a special effort to avoid the following four errors. These errors often cause misinterpretation and in turn create apparent contradictions.

1. Making a biblical statement more inclusive or more universal that the writer intended.
2. Applying a biblical statement incorrectly outside its own dispensation or its own specific circumstances.
3. Viewing a biblical statement from a certain theological position. When this is done, the biblical statement may mistakenly be seen as proof not only for one particular tenet of the theological position, but also as proof for other related tenets in that theological position. Then one of those other tenets is compared with another biblical statement and an apparent contradiction results.
4. Using the converse or inverse of a biblical statement and assuming that the converse or inverse is automatically true just because the biblical statement is true. (See the discussion of "Improper Inference" in chapter 13.)

In many instances, a very careful examination of the immediate and larger context of a biblical statement will be the key to resolving the apparent contradiction.

When you are unable to resolve an apparent contradiction, be satisfied to set the problem aside temporarily. It is far better to proceed prayerfully and deliberately and to suspend judgment for a while than to jump to a conclusion. You may feel that you have examined all the relevant facts and have considered every possible interpretation of the passages, but in some cases it may be years or even a lifetime before you become aware of another fact or interpretation which will allow you to resolve the problem.

13

Proper Reasoning

Many Christians fear reasoning, logic, and philosophy. They feel that the Christian is expected to substitute faith for rigorous mental activity. But such a view misrepresents both faith and reasoning. Jesus said, "You shall love the Lord your God ... with all your mind" (Matt. 22:37). Peter said, "Gird your minds for action" (1 Pet. 1:13). "God gave Solomon wisdom and very great discernment" (1 Kings 4:29), and Solomon said, "Acquire wisdom! Acquire understanding!" (Prov. 4:5). These and other passages indicate that God does want you to think and reason with your mind. A problem arises, of course, if you base your thinking on false assumptions (false premises, false presuppositions) to start with. You must not build your reasoning on "the tradition of men" and "the elementary principles of the world" (Col. 2:8) or on "your own understanding" (Prov. 3:5). But this does not mean that you should not reason. It means that you must be careful to base your reasoning on the proper starting points, namely, on "The fear of the Lord" (Prov. 1:7; 9:10) and on Christ (Col. 2:8).

Circular Reasoning on Unfounded Assumptions

In this error, the person begins with an unfounded assumption. He then interprets the scriptural evidence in light of his assumption with the result that his own assumption, rather than the evidence, determines his conclusion. This type of error is discussed at length in chapter 5.

Overgeneralization

To overgeneralize is a built-in human trait. We hear one or two politicians of a particular party speak and we generalize that all the people in that party hold similar views. We watch a few members of a certain ethnic group, and we characterize all members of that ethnic group according to the few. And we can easily make the same error in interpreting the Bible by examining a small part of the evidence and then feeling that we have arrived at the full truth. For example, we might read how one or two of the patriarchs reacted under stress and generalize that that is how all the patriarchs reacted under stress. We must avoid this error in reasoning by actively seeking all the relevant evidence. When we skip over any part of the evidence and jump to a conclusion, we often jump to the wrong conclusion.

Argument from Silence

It is poor reasoning to argue that an idea is true just because there is no biblical statement that the idea is false. Likewise, it is poor reasoning to argue that an idea is false just because there is no biblical statement that it is true. Such arguments are based on silence, that is, lack of evidence.

In many places the biblical records are much shorter than they might have been. The records of creation, the experiences of the patriarchs, the deeds of the kings, the life and ministry of Jesus, and the acts of the apostles are all extremely brief. This brevity, or selectivity, becomes obvious from just a casual reading. Also, John explicitly states this fact in connection with the life of Jesus when he notes that "there are also many other things which Jesus did, which if they were written in detail, I suppose that even the world itself would not contain the books which were written" (John 21:25; also see Acts 2:40). The Bible does not attempt to speak in full detail on every possible subject. Thus, when we find a silence in the Bible, we must be careful not to interpret that silence incorrectly. Lack of an approving statement is not in itself a disapproval. Likewise, lack of a disapproving statement is not in itself an approval.

Also, because of this brevity of the biblical record, we should not assign too much significance to the statistical analysis of the Bible. For instance, we may calculate that the apostles witnessed in one way in 80 percent of the incidents and in another way in 20 percent of the incidents. But we must remember that we do not really know how often the apostles actually witnessed in one way or the other. All we know is how often they witnessed in one way or the other *in those incidents which are recorded*, which may be only a small fraction of the actual witnessing incidents.

On the one hand, when the Bible is silent, our safest position may also be to be silent. On the other hand, we must not forget that even though the Bible may not explicitly address a certain topic, we are often able to apply relevant biblical principles to that topic and thus reach a conclusion.

Furthermore, there are some cases in which a silence in the Bible does in fact have more significance than in other cases. If there is a high degree of likelihood that something should be said on a certain topic, but nothing is said, then that silence becomes more significant.

For instance, in Acts 1:7 nothing is said about the Holy Spirit taking part in fixing times and dates. Only the Father is mentioned. This fact in itself is not an adequate basis for concluding that only the Father is responsible for determining times and dates. However, it is interesting to note that Jesus refers to the Holy Spirit in a previous discussion (verse 5), and more importantly, refers again to the Holy Spirit in the very next clause (verse 8). This makes it a little more likely that Jesus' omission of the Holy Spirit in verse 7 is meant to be instructive. If this section were intended as a list of the activities of the Father, then the omission of the Holy Spirit from verse 7 would be less noteworthy. But since it is not a listing of the Father's activities, and since the Holy Spirit is already an important part of the discussion, his omission from verse 7 seems to carry more weight in determining the unique functions of the Father and of the Holy Spirit. (Of course, comparing Acts 1:7 with other passages, such as Matthew 24:36 and Mark 13:32, is also crucial in settling this issue.)

Even though silence is usually a poor basis for an argument, there are times when the circumstances in a given context make the silence more significant and in turn make the silence a more valid basis for the argument.

Argument by Analogy

In an analogy, as in certain figures of speech (such as metaphor, simile, parable, and allegory), two things are compared for the purpose of illustrating or clarifying something about one of them. Even though analogies can illustrate a point which is known to be true, they cannot establish a point. *Analogies do not prove anything; they only clarify.* Thus, to argue by analogy is never a strong argument. For instance, in Matthew 13 Jesus illustrates some important facts about the spread of the word to different types of persons by drawing an analogy between that and sowing seed in various types of soil. It is a fact that different persons respond differently to the word, but that fact is not established because different soils produce different yields. That fact is merely clarified or illustrated by the analogy of the soils. Should we argue that since the soil makes no choice, people also do not really choose? Should we argue that since the soil's yield was measured numerically, numerical measurement is the way we should evaluate a person's response to the Word? Neither of these two arguments is sound, because no analogy can serve as a basis for establishing an idea as fact. Analogies can only illustrate a fact that is already established, and it should not be assumed that every aspect of the analogy is meant to illustrate every aspect of the truth with which it is being compared. Beware of argument by analogy.

Improper Inference

It is possible to twist a biblical statement without even being aware that you are changing its meaning. Taking careful note of the exact way in which the statement is expressed (that is, the form of the statement) can help you avoid this error. Many of the statements in the Bible can be put into the If-A-then-B form. This type of statement is known in the field of logic as a conditional proposition or a sequential proposition. Such a statement says that *if* (on the condition that) the first part of the statement (A, the antecedent) is true, *then* it necessarily follows that the second part of the statement (B, the consequent) is also true. For example, common knowledge about automobiles can easily be put into the If-A-then-B form.

	(If A)	(then B)
Conditional proposition:	If your car is out of gasoline,	then it will not run.

The above proposition is true; that is, the then-clause is true whenever the if-clause is true. And you are "safe" as long as you maintain the form of the statement. But when you begin to alter its form you may find that you have actually twisted it and changed its meaning. The three alterations in the form are known as (1) the converse, which interchanges the if-clause and the then-clause so that the statement reads If B, then A; (2) the inverse, which negates both clauses so that the statement reads If not A, then not B; and (3) the contrapositive, which interchanges and negates both clauses so that the statement reads If not B, then not A.

	If	then
Converse:	your car will not run,	it is out of gasoline.
Inverse:	If your car has gasoline,	then it will run.
Contrapositive:	If your car will run,	then it has gasoline.

Here is a very basic rule of logic: Even though a conditional proposition is true, *the converse and inverse of that proposition may be true or false.* (By the way, if the conditional proposition is true, the contrapositive is always true.) You can check this out easily by thinking through the automobile illustration above, or any other conditional proposition such as, "If you live in Illinois, then you live in the United States" or "If it is raining, then it is cloudy."

If this rule of logic is neglected in Bible interpretation, you may unintentionally twist some biblical statements. For example, Proverbs 18:22 can be stated in the If-A-then-B form.

Conditional
proposition: If   then
                     a man gets   he obtains the
                     married,   Lord's favor.

Some people might interpret this verse to mean that all men should marry *because God disapproves of celibacy.* But notice that such a viewpoint actually expresses the inverse of the original biblical proposition, and that inverse is not necessarily true.

Inverse: If   then
                     a man remains   he obtains the
                     single,   Lord's *dis*favor.

When handling biblical statements you must be very careful lest you twist a true statement into a not-necessarily-true statement and then build your beliefs on that twisted statement.

This illustrates only one of the many types of statements which always operate according to the rules of language and logic. You would be wise to read as much as possible in the field of logic. Biblical statements must not be handled carelessly.

Definition Versus Partial Description

A definition uses the word *is*. However, not every statement using "is" is a definition. A great deal of confusion can be created if a biblical statement using the word *is* is thought to be a definition when it is really only a partial description. For example, the following statements might appear to be definitions since they use "is," but they are merely partial descriptions.

> God is love. (1 John 4:8)
> The gospel . . . is the power of God for salvation to everyone who believes. (Rom. 1:16)
> Faith is the assurance of things hoped for, the conviction of things not seen. (Heb. 11:1)

The following two statements illustrate the distinction between definitions and partial descriptions.

Definition	Partial description
An automobile is a four-wheeled, self-propelled vehicle designed primarily to carry passengers.	An automobile is a modern convenience.

The partial description does not apply very many limitations. Thus, the complete predicate (the part of the statement beginning with "is") could easily refer to other things besides automobiles. For example, a telephone is also a modern convenience. On the other hand, the definition applies enough limitations so that the predicate can refer only to an automobile. In fact, the word *define* means "to limit," or "to set boundaries." A statement using "is" is not a definition unless the predicate applies enough limitations so that it can refer only to the subject of the statement.

In a definition the word *is* could be replaced by the word *equals,* whereas in a partial description the "is" would be replaced by "can be described as," or "has, as one of its characteristics, the characteristic of being."

Definition	**Partial description**
An automobile equals a four-wheeled, self-propelled vehicle designed primarily to carry passengers.	An automobile can be described as a modern convenience. Or, an automobile has, as one of its characteristics, the characteristic of being a modern convenience.

It is very important to determine when "is" means "equals," and when "is" means something else. For example, it would be quite inaccurate to say that "God is love" means "God equals love," when in reality love is only one of God's many characteristics.

14

Application

After we have discovered the teachings of the Bible, we must use those teachings in our lives.

> Be careful to do according to all that is written. (Josh. 1:8)

> Prove yourselves doers of the word, and not merely hearers who delude themselves. (Jas. 1:22)

> That you may be filled with the knowledge of His will . . . so that you may walk in a manner worthy of the Lord, to please Him in all respects . . . for the attaining of all steadfastness and patience. (Col. 1:9-11)

> The things you have learned and received and heard and seen in me, practice these things. (Phil. 4:9)

In fact, to gain Bible knowledge that has practical implications for your life, but not use that knowledge in your life, is a very serious matter indeed.

> To one who knows the right thing to do, and does not do it, to him it is sin. (Jas. 4:17)

Today, if you would hear His voice,/Do not harden
your hearts. (Ps. 95:7-8)

This sounds a warning to the person who, out of pride,
studies his Bible with a motive of showing off his vast
Bible knowledge, or to the person who, out of a desire for
recognition, studies his Bible with a motive of gaining
acceptance with those who value Bible study.

Many times a biblical teaching can be directly applied
in our lives. When the Bible states a general principle
which is relevant to us, we should begin living and acting according to that principle with, of course, the Holy
Spirit's help.

Other times, however, what we find in the Bible is not
a principle which is directly applicable to us, but an
example or a command which was directly applicable to
a certain person (or group) in a particular situation. His
specific actions might have been proper *for him in his
circumstances,* but we cannot necessarily apply them
directly in our circumstances, which are probably different than his. In these cases our task is to uncover the
general principle underlying this specific example or
command and then reapply that principle in our own circumstances. The general principle is transferable; the
specific applications may not be.

For instance, Jesus gave a specific command to his
disciples not to leave Jerusalem. Then he added, "You
shall be My witnesses both in Jerusalem, and in all
Judea and Samaria, and even to the remotest part of the
earth" (Acts 1:8). Certainly this command *in itself, as it
is worded here,* is not a general principle which we are to
apply directly to our situation, for if that were the case
we should all begin our witnessing in Jerusalem. We
need to uncover the general principle which determined

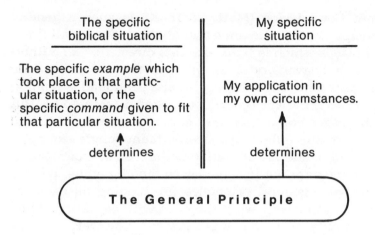

this command in that situation. Once that general principle is uncovered, we can then determine how it should be applied in our particular situation. However, uncovering the general principle is not an easy task. For instance, which of the following possible general principles was in Jesus' mind and determined the specific command he gave? Begin where you are. Or, begin where the most receptive group is. Or, begin in a large city. *Extreme care must be exercised so that we do not jump to a conclusion regarding the principles underlying specific biblical examples and commands.* Another interesting illustration of a biblical command which was given to fit specific circumstances is found in Jesus' command to his disciples *not* to tell people that he was the Messiah (Matt. 16:20).

Furthermore, there are varying degrees to which biblical examples and commands are binding on us. General spiritual principles are obviously binding since they can be applied in all places and at all times. The

Great Commission (Matt. 28:18-20) is such a general principle. Notice the universal applicability for all times and places which is built into this directive: "*all* authority . . . in heaven *and* on earth . . . *all* the nations . . . I am with you *always.*" Certainly such a command is binding on us, even though it was not spoken directly to us. But many other commands and examples are *less* binding on us for the following reasons. Many single examples and commands are situation-bound. Such examples or commands are not in themselves binding on us, but the underlying general principles *are* binding on us *if* we are able to discern what they are with certainty. When an example or command is repeated, however, it comes closer to being a general principle, especially if it is being repeated in varying circumstances. Also, although the examples of Jesus are always correct in the given situation, the examples of others are subject to error. The biblical writings of the prophets and apostles are inspired and thus errorless, but on some occasions their actions are poor examples for us (Ex. 18:13-26; Num. 20:7-12; 2 Sam. 11:1-27; Gal. 2:11-14; Acts 15:36-40). Thus, before making an application, we should ask the following questions:

1. Is this command in itself a general principle, or is it a situation-bound command?

2. What is the general principle underlying this specific command or example? How certain am I that I have uncovered the correct principle?

3. Is this the example of Christ or of someone else?

4. Is this a single example or command, or is it a repeated one? Are the situations in which it is repeated all alike, or are they varied?

This does not mean that we can simply ignore the single examples of the prophets or apostles. Even with these we must carefully evaluate the example or the command and attempt to discern how binding it is on us and what underlying principle it represents.

There are three other mistakes which are commonly made in regard to Bible application. The first mistake is actually the opposite of what has just been discussed. Just as it is improper to attempt to apply every example and every command to your own specific situation, it is also improper to dismiss every example and every command on the assumption that none of them is relevant to you today. We must remember that (1) many passages are relevant for all places and at all times since they are statements of general principles, and (2) every specific example and command which is intended for only one place and time is still based on a general principle which can be reapplied today. Philippians 2:2-3 is an example of a passage which is directly applicable today. To evade the application of such a passage on any so-called "cultural" grounds is to rationalize away one's only valid response to the Word of God and to frustrate the purpose for personal Bible study.

Another mistake is to think of the application of Scripture as a separate "method," often called the "devotional method." When this is done, it is very easy to think of application as merely one of several methods to choose from, so that you can perhaps use the "devotional method" on one passage or topic, but not on the next. Actually, personal application of Scripture is something which you should be willing and ready to do at all times, not merely when you have chosen to adopt the "devotional method." No one should put application out of mind simply because he is not currently using that "method."

Another mistake is to attempt to use a devotional

"method" or application "method" too soon—before you
have gone through all the hard work that is necessary to
ensure that you have the best possible interpretation of
the passage or topic. It is dangerous to apply a passage
in your life before working through the process of finding out exactly what the text says, and before being sure
of its true meaning. Personal application must be placed
where it belongs—*following* careful, systematic observation and reflective interpretation.

15

Where to Start

Before you study any particular Bible book or any particular Bible topic, you should have a bird's-eye view of the whole Bible.

Bird's-Eye View

The Bible *is* a large book, equal in length to perhaps two or three volumes of an encyclopedia. Thus, it helps to be able to see the basic overall organization of the Bible. The chart on pages 140-141 gives the main divisions of both Testaments. (If personal Bible study is completely new to you, you would be wise to take time out and memorize the books of the Bible in their proper order. Also memorize the categories, and which books make up each category.)

To get a bird's-eye view of the actual content of all the books of the Bible, follow the plan described below. This plan surveys the whole Bible in such a way that the content can be easily remembered and reviewed. Start with the Book of Genesis. As you read each chapter, write out a very brief summary of that chapter in your notebook. Your summary of each chapter might consist of a few phrases or a sentence or two. When you complete the fifty chapters in Genesis you will have the entire book condensed into two or three pages in your notebook.

Then read over your condensation, divide it into several
sections, and give a short title (one, two, or three words)
to each section. For example, Genesis easily divides into
five sections entitled Beginning Events (chaps.
1-11), Abraham (1,2—25), Isaac (25—26), Jacob (27—36), and
Joseph (37-50). Do the same for each book of the Bible.
(You may also want to memorize your section titles so
that you have a capsule of each book's content at your
fingertips.) When you finish the entire Bible you will be
able to think through its entire content, book by book, by
reviewing your section titles. Many people faithfully
read their Bible through every year, and this is a very
commendable practice. But since they do not record,
divide, title, and review, they may quickly forget most of
what they have read. They are left with a blur instead of
a clear bird's-eye view. The plan described above does
not take much longer than it takes to read through the
Bible, but the resulting benefits are far greater. In fact,
if you read three or four chapters every day, you can
complete your survey within one year. Then, of course,
it is beneficial to continue to read the Bible through on a
regular or periodic basis.

After you have a clear bird's-eye view of the whole
Bible, you are ready to focus in on more intensive Bible
study. However, you should not think in terms of dozens
of Bible study "methods." Instead, think in terms of *one
basic approach* which consistently employs the principles of proper Bible study already discussed in earlier
chapters. This one basic approach can begin, however,
at either of two basic starting points, book study or topic
study.

Book Studies

While complete book study will include topic study,
and while complete topic study will include book study,

book study is basic to topic study and, generally speaking, should come first. Book study should precede topic study for the following reasons. First, the Bible was written that way—in books rather than topically arranged. Indeed, some sections of some books are organized topically, but the Bible as a whole is not arranged for topical reference. Second, even when studying a topic, relevant passages from various books each need to be examined in their own immediate and larger context, and a thorough knowledge of the Bible, book by book, helps a great deal. Third, when studying topics it is necessary to bring some assumptions to the study for the necessary process of identifying relevant passages. This is unavoidable. Yet, since you need to constantly guard against *unfounded* assumptions, book study should come before topic study in order to ensure that the few assumptions which you must bring to the topic study are founded in your study of Bible books. Thus, *the study of Bible books lays a necessary foundation for the study of Bible topics.*

You will be tempted to launch into a study of one topic after another. After all, it seems like a quick road to Bible knowledge. It seems inviting to be able to say that you have studied everything that the Bible says on such and such a topic. And, of course, certain interesting and controversial topics catch our fancy. However, the person who is best equipped to study Bible topics is the person who has spent years studying Bible books. Therefore, discipline yourself to establish a schedule of Bible book study first, and as a general rule, let the topic studies wait until later.

Here are some suggestions for your first few book studies.

1. Philippians
2. Mark
3. 1 John

BIBLE BOOKS BY CATEGORIES
(according to their arrangement in the English Bible)

OLD TESTAMENT – 39 Books

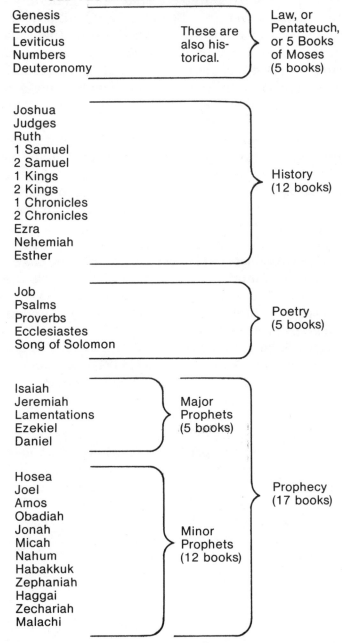

Genesis
Exodus
Leviticus
Numbers
Deuteronomy

These are also historical.

Law, or Pentateuch, or 5 Books of Moses (5 books)

Joshua
Judges
Ruth
1 Samuel
2 Samuel
1 Kings
2 Kings
1 Chronicles
2 Chronicles
Ezra
Nehemiah
Esther

History (12 books)

Job
Psalms
Proverbs
Ecclesiastes
Song of Solomon

Poetry (5 books)

Isaiah
Jeremiah
Lamentations
Ezekiel
Daniel

Major Prophets (5 books)

Hosea
Joel
Amos
Obadiah
Jonah
Micah
Nahum
Habakkuk
Zephaniah
Haggai
Zechariah
Malachi

Minor Prophets (12 books)

Prophecy (17 books)

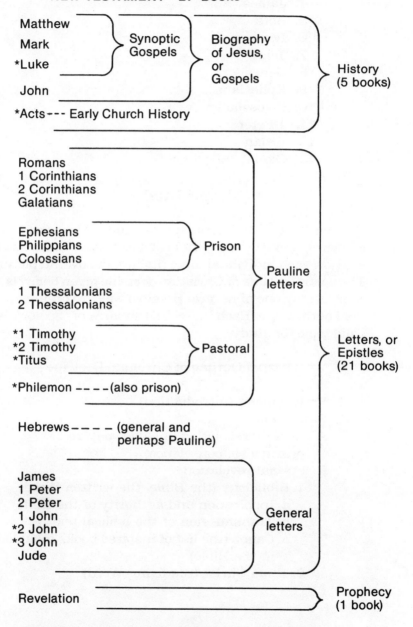

NEW TESTAMENT – 27 Books

Matthew
Mark
*Luke
} Synoptic Gospels
} Biography of Jesus, or Gospels
} History (5 books)

John

*Acts --- Early Church History

Romans
1 Corinthians
2 Corinthians
Galatians

Ephesians
Philippians
Colossians
} Prison
} Pauline letters

1 Thessalonians
2 Thessalonians

*1 Timothy
*2 Timothy
*Titus
} Pastoral

*Philemon – – – – (also prison)

} Letters, or Epistles (21 books)

Hebrews – – – – (general and perhaps Pauline)

James
1 Peter
2 Peter
1 John
*2 John
*3 John
Jude
} General letters

Revelation
} Prophecy (1 book)

*These New Testament books were written to individuals.

    4. James
    5. Acts
    6. Romans
    7. John
    8. Genesis
    9. Ephesians
  10. Colossians
  11. 1 Peter
  12. Isaiah
  13. Daniel

Topic Studies

When you finally get into topical study, it is good to have an overview of the whole field of theology so that you can see how each individual topic fits into the overall picture. The partial outline of Christian doctrine given below is, of course, only one of several possible ways to organize the field of theology. Each individual subarea of theology is a valid topic for study.

Partial Outline of Christian Doctrine

   I. Prologomena (Introduction)
  II. Revelation
    A. General revelation (includes nature, providence, conscience)
    B. Special revelation
      1. Bibliology (the Bible, the written Word)
        a. Inspiration and authority of the Bible
        b. Transmission of the biblical text
        c. Canon (the list of inspired books included in the Bible)
      2. Jesus Christ (the living Word)

III. Theology Proper (God)
    A. Nature of God
        1. Personalness of God
        2. The Trinity
    B. Names of God
    C. Attributes of God (holiness, justice, love, grace, mercy, etc.)
    D. Decrees of God
        1. Sovereignty
        2. Creation
    E. God the Father
IV. Angelology (Angels)
    A. Angels (unfallen)
    B. Satan and demons
V. Christology (Jesus Christ)
    A. Person of Christ
        1. His humanity
            a. Incarnation
            b. Virgin conception
        2. His deity and preexistence
    B. Work of Christ
        1. His sinless life
        2. His substitutionary death
        3. His resurrection and ascension
        4. His present ministry
VI. Pneumatology (The Holy Spirit)
    A. Personalness of the Holy Spirit
    B. Deity of the Holy Spirit
    C. Work of the Holy Spirit
VII. Anthropology (Man)
    A. Origin of man
    B. Nature of man
        1. His material part
        2. His immaterial part

   C. Fall of Man
   D. Hamartiology (sin)
VIII. Soteriology (Salvation)
   A. God's provisions (includes foreknowledge,
      election, predestination, calling, redemption,
      reconciliation, propitiation, regeneration,
      justification, adoption, sanctification,
      glorification, etc.)
   B. Man's response (repentance and faith)
      1. Eternal security (perseverance of the saints)
   C. Christian living
IX. Ecclesiology (the Church)
   A. The universal church
   B. The local church
 X. Eschatology (Last Things)
   A. Individual eschatology (includes heaven and
      hell)
   B. General eschatology (includes the return of
      Christ, millennium, eternal state)
XI. Apologetics:Systematic argumentation in defense
                 of the teachings of Christianity. Deals
                 particularly with the existence of a
                 personal God and the reliability of the
                 Bible.

   Each of the topics in the following list should be viewed
in relation to the above outline of doctrine. None of these
topics should be studied alone, but each should be studied
after, or along with, a study of the related subareas of
theology.

Partial List of Areas of Christian Living

   1. Assurance of salvation
   2. Lordship of Christ

3. Good works; obedience

4. Dedication, or Spirit-led living and victory over sin; filling of the Holy Spirit

5. Temptation; dealing with Satan

6. Maintaining fellowship with God (confession of sin, yielding to the Holy Spirit, etc.)

7. Using God's Word

8. Finding God's will (guidance)

9. Worship

10. Closeness to God, or the Lord's presence

11. Love for God and others

12. Faith (trust in God)

13. Grace

14. Prayer

15. Gratitude

16. Inner life; attitudes; motivation

17. Joy; peace; fear; sorrow; worry; discouragement (feelings and emotions)

18. Baptism

19. Pride; humility; self-acceptance

20. Speech

21. Liberty

22. Stronger—weaker brother

23. Thought-life; lusting

24. Honesty; lying

25. Separation; worldliness

26. God's discipline

27. Witnessing

28. Fellowship with other Christians; responsibilities to other Christians

29. Spiritual gifts

30. Patience; anger; self-control

31. Gossip

32. Judging

33. Forgiving others

34. False teachers
35. Husband-wife relationships
36. Parent-child relationships
37. Care of one's body
38. Citizenship
39. Stewardship; money; tithing; business dealings
40. Death

There are many, many other topics, such as the study of the lives of certain Bible characters, as well as all the controversial topics which come up in discussions again and again. You will be wise to avoid jumping into the study of one controversial area after another until you have grounded yourself well in the content of the Bible books and in the more basic topics of the Bible. Here are some suggestions for your first few topical studies.

1. The content of the gospel message (the plan of salvation)
2. Assurance of salvation
3. Prayer
4. Speech

16

Other Practical Matters

This chapter considers several practical details which have not been mentioned so far. Suggestions are given regarding time and place, books, choosing a translation, and how to relate DBD to your quiet time, Bible class, and Bible memorization.

Time and Place

Personal Bible study takes time. If you do not value personal Bible study very much—if you place it low among your priorities—you may try to *find* time for it. But if you value personal Bible study greatly you will *make* time. Once you have decided to set aside some other activities, you will need to work out a number of practical details in order to make your Bible study time most profitable.

Plan to set aside larger blocks of time. Do not try to do your Bible study in five or ten minute snatches. Depth study requires longer periods of concentration. Also, plan to study during a time of the day when you are alert. Everyone is different. Some people's minds are wide awake very early in the morning. Others can think most clearly late at night. You will be wise to plan your day so that your routine tasks come during your duller hours and your Bible study comes during your sharpest hours. Even though longer periods of concentration will usually work best, at times you might find it helpful to give your mind a rest for a while so that you can return to your study refreshed. Also try to choose a time when you can expect no interruptions.

The place in which you study is also important. Find a place where there will be no distractions and no interruptions. You should also have good lighting, good ventilation, and a desk arrangement in which your Bibles and aids are within arm's reach.

You may never find a time and place as ideal as those just described. Nevertheless, whatever your circumstances, you should plan a time and place for your Bible study that will help you *concentrate* best.

Books

You do not need a lot of expensive books in order to begin, but a few basics are essential. Of course, you need one or more **Bibles**. It is best to have just one or two good translations which you use as your basic study Bibles for most of your reading and close study, plus a few other translations for survey reading and for comparison. (Guidelines for choosing a translation are given in the next section of this chapter.)

You should also have a **notebook** for recording your observations, interpretations, questions, and many other things. A notebook which uses standard 8½ x 11″ paper is best. It should be a loose-leaf notebook so that you can easily rearrange the pages, and so that you can neatly remove your notes when you have completed a study in order to file them under the appropriate book or topic in your file.

The importance of writing out your thoughts during Bible study cannot be overemphasized. In Bible study you should never read without thinking, and never think without writing. Writing out your thoughts will help you in three ways. First, it will force you to make sure that your thoughts are clear enough to be written down. When we try to write out our ideas, we often find that we need to rethink them and unravel them before they can actually be put into writing. Second, the mere exercise of writing out our thoughts helps impress them on our memory so that they can be recalled more quickly and accurately later. Third, months or years later you will probably be surprised to read how much you had discovered and thought through which is by then forgotten. You will then be able to review and build on your previous efforts without having to redo a lot of work. An old proverb states that the strongest memory is weaker than the palest ink.

As a general rule, do not mark up your Bible. Some people clutter up the text in their Bibles by underlining words, filling in verses with colored pencils, drawing circles and arrows in the text, or writing notes in the margins. Indeed, such marks are handy at the moment. However, in the future they may hinder your discovery of *all* that the passage has to say. These marks may become a distraction, making it difficult to see any more than what you noticed the first time around. Avoid quickly marking up the text itself, although you may find it helpful to make note of your major divisions and subdivisions and their titles in the margin. While you are studying a passage, it is best to study from a "clean" copy of the text. Then *after* you have completed your study of the passage, you may want to make a few, carefully selected, key notations in the text itself.

You should also have a good **English dictionary** handy. Use it often, even when you think you understand a word. You may be surprised when you find that your usage of a certain term differs from standard usage.

A **large concordance** is indispensable, especially for topical study of the Bible. Many Bibles include a concordance at the back, but such concordances list only some of the words in the Bible; and under the words they do include, only some of the references where those words occur are listed. Thus, a large concordance is needed, such as Young's *Analytical Concordance to the Bible,* or *Strong's Exhaustive Concordance of the Bible.* These concordances are based on the wording of the King James Version of the Bible. If you are using the *New American Standard Bible,* the *New American Standard Exhaustive Concordance of the Bible* is available. Be sure to read the prefaces, introductions, directions, in your concordance, where you will find valuable information on how to get the most out of your concordance.

It is also important to have a set of Bible **maps**. Many of the Bible dictionaries include an atlas of Bible maps, which is sufficient in most cases. Or, separate Bible atlases can be purchased. Keep your maps handy and use them often.

All of the aids mentioned above are noninterpretive aids. It is also helpful to use interpretive aids, especially to compare your findings with the findings of others. The more common interpretive aids can be divided into two main types: (1) annotated Bibles, Bible commentaries, and the like, which are organized around the books of the Bible in order, and (2) Bible dictionaries, systematic theologies, and the like, which are organized mainly according to Bible topics. Annotated Bibles such as *The New Scofield Reference Bible,* the *Harper Study Bible,* and the *Holman New American Standard Study Bible* include such helps as cross-references, footnotes, introductions, outlines for each book, a brief concordance, maps, etc. One-volume commentaries such as *The Wycliffe Bible Commentary, The New Bible Commentary: Revised,* and *The Teacher's Bible Commentary* are handy in that they cover all the books of the Bible. Multivolume commentaries such as the *New International Commentary* series, *The Broadman Bible Commentary,* and *The Layman's Bible Book Commentary* usually devote one volume to each book of the Bible and are thus able to go into much greater depth than one-volume commentaries. Bible dictionaries such as *The Zondervan Pictorial Bible Dictionary, The New Bible Dictionary,* or the *Davis Dictionary of the Bible,* and Bible encyclopedias such as *The Zondervan Pictorial Encyclopedia of the Bible* or the *Wycliffe Bible Encyclopedia* cover a wide range of biblical and theological topics alphabetically arranged. Systematic theologies such as Thiessen's *Introductory Lectures in Systematic Theology* cover theological topics logically arranged. Books such as *Christian Doctrine* by Walter Thomas Conner and *Doctrines of the Christian Religion* by William W. Stevens are similar sources. Dictionaries of theology such as *Baker's Dictionary of Theology* and *The New International Dictionary of New Testament Theology* cover theological words and topics alphabetically arranged.

Choosing a Translation

The New Testament was originally written in Greek, and the Old Testament was originally written mostly in Hebrew. Our chief concern here, however, is the study of the English Bible. You do not need to know Greek and Hebrew to do meaningful and rewarding personal Bible study; but, of course, a knowledge of these languages is very helpful, especially for the professional who plans to teach or minister full-time.

Which translation of the Bible is best for personal Bible study? *No translation is perfect,* but there are many good translations available. When you choose a translation you should keep these four factors in mind.

First, the translation you choose should be an *accurate* translation—one which faithfully conveys in good, readable English the same ideas and meanings that were conveyed in the original languages. Of all the factors discussed in this section, this matter of accuracy is by far the most important factor in choosing a translation.

Of course, it must be recognized that every translation of the Bible is interpretive to at least some degree. Translation from any language to any other language is not merely a mechanical process of substituting the words of one language for the words of the other language. Various languages do not have the same structure, the same vocabulary, or the same idioms, so translation in a computer-like fashion, merely substituting word for word, is impossible. Instead, the translator must translate thought for thought, idea for idea, emphasis for emphasis, meaning for meaning, which mere mechanical word-for-word translation could never adequately accomplish. Because the translator must interpret the original before he can translate it, every translation of the Bible is, to at least a small degree, interpretive.

While it is true that even the more literal, or the more "strict," translations are somewhat interpretive, some versions go far beyond strict translations and purposely attempt to expand and clarify the wording for the reader. Such versions are more properly called "paraphrases" or "expanded translations." Because they include additional words and phrases in order to make better sense, they also require more interpretation than is required in strict translation. When there is ambiguity in the original languages of the Bible, the strict translator will retain that ambiguity rather than adding his own interpretation to his translation. On the other hand, the paraphraser will add his own interpretation in an attempt to clarify the ambiguity for the reader. As he does so he is guided more by his theological position than by the original text. This additional clarity may seem like an advantage to the person who is reading the passage for the first time. However, for careful inductive study of the Bible, a more literal translation is best. Paraphrased versions and expanded translations, being moderately interpretive aids, should be used later in your study procedure for comparison, but for your own careful scrutiny of a passage you should use a relatively literal translation.

A second factor to keep in mind when choosing a translation is that the translation should use *current* English. Unfortunately, many words in the King James Version of the Bible have changed their meanings since that translation was made in 1611 (over three and one-half centuries ago). Examples of such word changes can be easily found by referring to *What You Should Know About Bible Translations* by G. Christian Weiss, and *God's Word into English* by Dewey M. Beegle. It is misleading in everyday communication to use one word when we mean something quite different. It is just as misleading to use a translation containing some words which, because of the gradual changes in the English language over a long period of time, no longer accurately represent the ideas in the original manuscripts of the Bible. This problem is largely overcome in *The New Scofield Reference Bible* and *The New King James Bible* which make such word changes as are necessary to bring the expressions of the King James Version in line with current English.

There are some who favor the King James Version because they feel that the textus receptus (the manuscript type from which the New Testament of the King James Version was translated) is either identical to the original manuscripts, or closer to the original manuscripts than any other manuscript type. Both of these viewpoints are rejected by the general consensus of conservative Bible scholars. Although this is a matter for the experts (the textual critics) to resolve, and is beyond the scope of this guidebook, one observation is helpful here. The textus receptus and the other manuscript types are not vastly different from each other. In the New Testament differences in wording are found roughly at a rate of only four words or phrases per chapter (plus two longer passages, Mark 16:9-20 and John 7:53 to 8:11). Furthermore, the *significant* differences in wording—differences that add to the meaning or change the basic meaning of a particular passage— are far less frequent. These significant differences (not including the two longer passages mentioned above) could all be contained on one or two pages. *No basic doctrine is altered in any way.* For all practical Bible study purposes, the Greek text underlying the New Testament of the King James Version and the Greek text underlying most modern translations are nearly identical, and the same can be said for the Hebrew texts underlying the Old Testament.

The third factor to keep in mind is that the Bible you choose should be a committee translation rather than a translation made by one person. The wealth of scholarship in a balanced committee should obviously produce a better translation, all other factors being equal. You can quickly tell by reading the introduction in most translations whether it was made by an individual or by a committee.

Fourth, the Bible you choose should not be an annotated Bible. It should be printed without cross-references, outlines, headings, or interpretive notes added to the text. (Such interpretive notes are not to be confused with alternate translations and variations in manuscript readings which are noted in the margins or at the foot of the page in most Bibles, and which are noninterpretive.) Interpretive additions are not inspired. It is important to avoid dependence on such interpretive additions, especially in the earlier phases of proper Bible study procedure, as explained in chapter 4. One of the ways to do this is to avoid the use of an annotated Bible as your main study Bible.

There are a number of excellent versions of the Bible which could be used as your basic study Bible. However, two are especially recommended: the *New American Standard Bible* and the *New International Version*. Of these two, the *New American Standard Bible* is more literal, but also less readable. Thus, an excellent combination would be to use the *New International Version* as your basic Bible for survey reading and first readings of a particular passage, and then to use the *New American Standard Bible* as your basic Bible for close study of the passages.

Having a few other translations will also prove helpful for survey reading and for making comparisons, passage by passage. Other translations which are good for this purpose include *The Modern Language Bible: The New Berkeley Version* and the Revised Standard Version. Since no single translation is perfect, you should regularly compare the wording of the passage you are studying in a few different translations. At the same time, however, avoid the extreme of spending the majority of your study time jumping from one translation to another.

In order to become more familiar with the different versions, be sure to read the prefaces, introductions, and other front matter in your various Bibles.

DBD and Other Common Practices

Many Christians are involved in three common practices which supply Bible input: (1) the daily quiet time or private devotional period; (2) the weekly discussions of the Bible at Sunday School classes or home Bible study groups; and (3) Bible memorization. Each of these practices is very beneficial in furthering one's knowledge of the Bible and thus laying a foundation for growth in one's Christian life. A question naturally arises regarding the relationship between DBD and these three practices.

Your daily quiet time should include at least the following two basic elements: Bible study and prayer. DBD does not replace the Bible study which you do as part of your quiet time; nor does the Bible study which you do as part of your quiet time replace DBD. DBD is a particular *way* of studying the Bible, and thus it is not in competition with your quiet time at all. Rather, DBD should be the way you study your Bible *during* your quiet time. This requires, of course, that ample time be set aside for your quiet time. DBD is the basic approach you should use in studying the Bible both during your quiet time and at other times as well.

You should also take advantage of a small Bible study group or Sunday School class. Again, DBD does not replace Bible study groups or Sunday School classes; nor do they replace DBD. The best pattern is to maintain *both* individual and group study on a regular basis. You will be able to share your findings and applications with others, and they will be able to stimulate your mind with topics, questions, possible interpretations, and their own applications that will enhance your own Christian life and your personal Bible study. The Bible says that we are to *"stimulate one another* to love and good deeds, not forsaking our own assembling together . . . but *encouraging one another"* (Heb. 10:24-25), and small Bible study groups and Sunday School classes are ideal places to do this. Whatever the group, encourage those who are studying the Bible with you to discover the teachings of the Bible directly. In fact, a good pattern would be to plan each week's Bible discussion around the steps in the DBD procedures explained in the next two chapters. Each individual would be expected to use DBD on his own, and then he would be prepared each week to contribute "intelligently" to the discussion. Group discussions of a Bible passage are most helpful when they follow, rather than precede, each individual's private study of that passage.

The third common practice is Bible memorization. Many Christians recommend Bible memorization for children, but it is just as valuable for adults. Again, DBD does not replace Bible memorization; nor does Bible memorization replace DBD. The most meaningful pattern would be to memorize Bible passages *after* you have studied the passage according to the principles and procedures of DBD. A passage which is memorized merely for the sake of memorizing one more passage, and which is isolated from its immediate context, is often memorized in a mechanical, meaningless, rote fashion. The danger is that such passages are often misunderstood, and then misapplied. It is much better to memorize passages which have already become meaningful through the use of DBD on a Bible book or Bible topic. When a passage comes to your attention through some other means, and you desire to memorize it, it is important to thoroughly study that passage in context in order to guard against misinterpreting or misapplying it.

17

The Procedure for Studying Books

Before explaining the procedure for studying the books of the Bible, something needs to be said about the danger of procedures without meaning.

Procedures Versus Meaning

As you glance through chapters 17 and 18 and see the detailed procedures, you might easily feel that DBD seems quite complex. However, you would be wise to follow these procedures precisely the way they are described. From the experience of this writer and of many others you can be assured that DBD works!

On the one hand, you are asked to try these procedures exactly as they are spelled out in these two chapters. Use chapter 17 on several books, and use chapter 18 on several topics. On the other hand, no one is expected to follow these procedures in every detail for the rest of his life. Once you come to appreciate the basic DBD approach and have tried the procedures, you will be able to supplement them and modify them without violating the basic approach and the important principles on which the procedures are built. You may want to adjust the procedures to suit your own personality, abilities, and purposes in personal Bible study. Give DBD a try, but treat it for what it is—a tool—your servant and not your master.

It would be quite easy for you to work through all the procedures and still not study the Bible *with understanding*. It is possible for a person to engage in all of these procedures and merely go through the motions of Bible study with his mind disengaged. Always be alert and thinking. It is of greatest importance that you approach the Bible, not merely with mechanical gimmicks, but with the most basic approach of all: *reading and studying for meaning*. If you approach the Bible with the goal of producing a neat outline, drawing a beautiful chart, finding hidden clues, or any other mechanical gimmick, you may be able to do all those things, yet you may never really understand the passage you are working with. Furthermore, if you begin by looking for special answers or hidden clues, you may easily overlook the message that is right there in plain sight. Certainly the procedures just mentioned have a proper place, but such procedures must not be allowed to become ends in themselves. For instance, outlining is a legitimate procedure, but you have not necessarily determined the meaning of a passage merely because you have outlined the passage. Outlining is only a tool to aid you in finding the structure of a passage, and thus a hint of the meaning of the passage. But sometimes an outline can hide the meaning of the passage rather than reveal it. Read and study *for meaning*. Step back and look at the purpose and significance of the entire passage instead of limiting yourself to a spider's view. *Continually relate every detail you see to the main thrust or the central idea of the passage.* Don't let the details keep you from seeing the explicit teachings of the passage. Don't cover up the meaning with insensitive, mechanical procedures. Bible study must operate in the realm of meaning and not merely in the realm of activity.

You will be better able to see the end from the beginning if you read through this entire chapter before you begin to put any of the procedure into operation.

The Procedure

The eight steps in the procedure for studying books of the Bible are:

1. Pray	5. Examine topics
2. Survey	6. Synthesize
3. Divide	7. Compare
4. Scrutinize	8. Apply

This procedure balances a focus on the details with a focus on the book as a whole. Bible study must involve a great deal of careful, objective, detailed observation. But examining details is only one side of the coin. You must also be able to see the large picture all at once. In other words, look at the book panoramically as well as microscopically. Using just one type of search gives an incomplete picture. Seeing the whole, on the one hand, and scrutinizing the details, on the other hand, are *both* necessary.

For instance, which man has a more complete view of a large forest preserve, the helicopter pilot or the hiker? Obviously the pilot sees some things the hiker does not, and the hiker sees some things the pilot does not. So neither man's view of the forest preserve is complete. However, the hiker can be helped a great deal by taking a ride in the helicopter before going on a hike. He will then be able to orient himself more quickly when he is on the ground. Each individual trail will be better appreciated as it is understood in relation to other trails and the entire forest preserve, and the hiker will be less likely to get lost. Likewise, with literature, you should survey an entire book before you engage in a detailed study of any particular section. Your understanding of each section will be enhanced as you are able to see its relation to the other sections and to the trends of thought and emphases of the whole book. What otherwise might become a confusing forest of details can become much more meaningful.

In the study of a Bible book, a third component is also needed. After the details of each section of the book have been thoroughly scrutinized, it is necessary to put all the parts back together again to review the whole. Thus, your pattern in Bible book study should include first a look at the whole, then the parts, then the whole again. Of course, the eight steps listed above are in keeping with this pattern since they include step 2 (the whole), steps 3, 4, and 5 (the parts), and step 6 (the whole again).

Step 1—Pray

Pray. Does it really help? Before you pray you may want to think about some of the promises regarding God's Word, some of the promises regarding prayer, and some of the examples of prayer, such as 2 Timothy 3:15-17; Joshua 1:8; James 1:5; Matthew 7:7-11; John 14:13-14; Psalms 1:1-3; 19:7-11; 119:18,27,33-34,73,105-112,124-125,129-136,144,169-176.

Continue to pray with each of the following steps, every time you study your Bible. Pray each day before, during, and after you study. Ask for help in understanding, wisdom in application, etc.

Step 2—Survey

Survey the whole book. During the first few times through the book read it swiftly, and each time you read it through read it in one sitting without interruption. Ignore the chapter and verse divisions. Read the book in several different translations. Sometimes read it silently, sometimes aloud. Do *not* look for any particular details during these first several readings. Instead read for overall message and general impact. Record these first general impressions in your notebook.

Then as you continue to read through the book, record the following in your notebook.

1. Writer, place from which the book originated (locate on a map), and when the book was written (before or after what key historical events).

2. Recipients, and place of destination (locate on a map).

3. When the main events described in the book took place (before or after what key historical events).

4. Occasion of writing (events or circumstances which prompted the writing of the book), purpose for writing.

5. Type of literature (mainly historical, didactic, hortatory, poetic, apocalyptic, etc., or a combination of these), general style, tone (atmosphere or spirit), and other characteristics of the book. How did the writer feel when he wrote the book?

6. Main thrust(s) (basic message, central theme, repeated emphases).

7. Any major divisions which are obvious at this point.

Be sure to record all appropriate references (book name, chapter number, and verse numbers) in your notes.

When you find that one of the above items is not explicitly stated in the book, make note of that fact. Then record any relevant observations (with references) on which you might base a conclusion regarding that item. Be sure to keep your observations and your interpretations separate in your thinking and to state your degree of certainty when you record your conclusions.

At this point you should study more about the background of the book. You will recall that a Bible passage should be interpreted in the light of its historical and cultural setting. Thus, you will want to learn everything you can about the key historical and cultural items in the book. Such items include the key cities and their inhabitants, countries and their inhabitants, other groups of people, historical events, and common cultural practices that are mentioned in the book. For example, if you are studying one of the letters in the New Testament, one of the items you should learn about is the city in which the recipients of the letter lived and the inhabitants of that city—Rome, Corinth, Galatia, Ephesus, Philippi, Colossae, or Thessalonica. If you are studying one of the Old Testament prophets, you should find out all you can about the main cities or countries mentioned by the prophet.

Obviously, cities and countries should be located on a map, and you should find out as much as you can about geographical settings which you think might help you understand the text better. Check the time period represented by the map to be sure that you are using a map which matches the general date of the events you are studying.

Information about each of the key historical and cultural items should be researched in the following order. First, take note of everything that the book itself says about that item. Second, use your large concordance to uncover all the other biblical references to that item, and thus find out everything that the rest of the Bible says about it. Third, research additional information which comes from secular history and archaeology by looking up the item in a few Bible dictionaries or Bible encyclopedias. If, for instance, you are studying the Book of Philippians, you will immediately locate Philippi on a map of the first-century Mediterranean world or a map of Paul's missionary journeys. Then you should (1) take note of everything that the Book of Philippians says about Philippi; (2) look up "Philippi" in your large concordance to find out what other Bible passages (especially those in the Book of Acts) say about Philippi; and finally (3) look up a few articles on the city of Philippi in some Bible dictionaries or Bible encyclopedias to see what additional historical and archaeological findings might help you understand the city and its people. Articles on the city of Philippi will probably focus on the geographical, historical, and civil aspects of the city. Articles on the Book of Philippians will obviously be much more interpretive of the text, and you should keep that fact in mind if you decide to read them at this point in your study.

You should then follow the same threefold process in researching other key historical and cultural items about whatever book you are studying.

Step 3—Divide

Divide the book into major divisions. Do not force any preconceived types of divisions onto the book (such as "introduction, body, conclusion"). Do not look for any certain number of divisions. Instead, *look for natural divisions*. In other words, let the book divide itself. Look for indications of division which are built right into the text, such as a transitional phrase or a summary statement, a change to a new subject, a change in the location of the action, a change of persons being discussed, a gap in the time sequence, or a change in the literary form. This does not mean that every such change indicates a new major division of the book, but you should notice all such changes as you attempt to find the divisions which fit the book in the most natural way. Also, look for divisions which have a definite relationship to the main thrust of the book and the purpose of the book. Then give each major division a short, descriptive title (perhaps four or five words) which will help you remember its content.

Subdivide the major divisions and give your subdivisions titles. Continue by subdividing again and giving titles until you are down to *Immediate Context Units* (ICU). An ICU may sometimes be the same as a paragraph of the text, or it may include two or more very closely related paragraphs. Also, an ICU may begin within one paragraph and/or end within a different paragraph. The length of an ICU depends solely on how closely related the paragraphs or parts of paragraphs are to each other. A typical ICU may be approximately one-half chapter in length, although many will be longer and many will be shorter. Again, your subdivisions and ICUs should be chosen according to the natural divisions found right in the text. It will help you find these natural divisions if you take careful note of both the grammatical structure of the text and the progression of thought running through the text. Titles for ICUs should be descriptive, brief (perhaps two or three words), and chosen specifically to bring the content of the ICU back to your mind. Do not give the same title to two ICUs.

Longer books may end up with major divisions, subdivisions, further subdivisions, and then ICUs. Shorter books may end up with only one major "division" and only a few ICUs.

Construct either a chart or a preliminary outline giving the titles and references for all of your major divisions, subdivisions, and ICUs. Your chart or outline will, of course, probably be revised several times during the rest of your study. A book which ends up with two major divisions, several subdivisions, and a few ICUs in most of the subdivisions could be charted somewhat like the sample chart on the next page. Although various types of charts could be used (some running vertically, some horizontally, some diagonally, etc.), the important things for the chart to display are (1) the whole book at a glance; (2) the titles and references for each major division, subdivision, and ICU; and (3) the relative length of each division. A chart composed of closed rectangles gives the false impression that each division is an isolated unit. It is better to draw an open chart, as illustrated, to display the fact that there is a flow of events or an idea developing throughout the book, and that no division should ever be thought of as separated from the others. After you have completed your outline or chart, note which subjects or events the author dwells on at length, and which subjects or events are treated as incidental. This will give you further hints as to the purpose and main thrust of the book.

Step 4—Scrutinize

Scrutinize, analyze, and meditate on each ICU long and hard, attacking it from twelve different angles. Do not carry out any of these twelve operations hastily. Careful scrutiny, analysis, and meditation require time and concentration. Examine. Reflect. Ponder. Be patient.

The twelve operations are:

1. Read for meaning.
2. Respace the text.
3. Outline the ICU.
4. Note the function of this ICU.
5. Ask six standard questions.
6. Note grammatical details.
7. Identify relationships.
8. Alter the wording.
9. Paraphrase the ICU.
10. List the main teachings.
11. Condense the ICU.
12. Quiz, etc.

As you carry out each of these twelve operations, be

The Book of _____

1:1-4 Title (Opening/Greeting/Introduction/etc.)	

1:4 to 6:9 Title of Major Division	1:4-40 Title of Subdivision	1:4-15 Title of ICU
		1:16-32 Title of ICU
		1:33-40 Title of ICU
	2:1 to 4:4 Title of Subdivision	2:1 to 3:7 Title of ICU
		3:8 to 4:4 Title of ICU
	4:5-23 Title of Subdivision	4:5-23 Title of ICU (same as title of subdivision since there is only one ICU)
	4:24 to 6:9 Title of Subdivision	4:24-37 Title of ICU
		5:1-14 Title of ICU
		5:15-38 Title of ICU
		6:1-9 Title of ICU
6:10 to 11:31 Title of Major Division	6:10 to 9:31 Title of Subdivision	6:10-20 Title of ICU
		6:21 to 7:2 Title of ICU
		7:3-40 Title of ICU
		8:1 to 9:5 Title of ICU
		9:6-31 Title of ICU
	9:32 to 11:31 Title of Subdivision	9:32 to 10:37 Title of ICU
		11:1-16 Title of ICU
		11:17-31 Title of ICU

11:32-35 Title (Close/etc.)	

sure to write out all of your observations, interpretations, and questions in your notebook. (Review the four suggestions regarding making observations in ch. 8.) To help keep your notes organized, you may want to put your observations on forms like the one on the next page. Number your observations consecutively so that you can refer to them easily by number when you write out your interpretations. Not all observations will have corresponding interpretations. However, every interpretation must have at least one corresponding observation on which it is based. Whenever possible, write out your interpretation directly across from the observation(s) on which it is based. Whenever you write out a question, look again at the entire ICU to see if the answer is there. If not, list the several alternatives which you feel might be good potential answers to the question.

1. Begin making observations on the ICU simply by *carefully reading the ICU for meaning.* Read the ICU *as a unit* (as a whole, from beginning to end without stopping) *many times.* Then read it again as a unit several times in different translations. Each time you read it, try to read it as though it were your first time! Take time to meditate on the meaning and the *main point* of the ICU.

Many people have trouble concentrating on what they are reading. They forget the previous sentence while they are reading the present sentence. To overcome this lack of memory and concentration, develop the habit of holding a summary of the essence of the previous sentences consciously in your mind as you read each new sentence. In this way you can readily identify the *development of the thought* in each ICU. This takes hard mental work, but it is also very important if you are going to read for meaning.

Reference _____ Title _____ Page _____			
(translation _____)		_____ Date _____	
Verses	Observations	Resultant Interpretations and Questions	Practical Applications

←— *(1⅜") —✕— (2⅞") —✕— (2⅞") —✕— (1⅜") —→

*These measurements refer to the size you should make your columns on your study sheets, not to the size of the columns in this book.

Don't overlook the obvious teachings of the passage. If you begin your search by looking for hidden clues or minute details, you may miss what is right on the surface. The message that is in plain view is what you should see first. Also, *put yourself into the situation* by trying to think as the writer, original readers, the persons mentioned in the text might have. Imagine that you are present to see and hear all that is done and said. Visualize each event and situation. Take part in the action and identify and empathize with each character in turn, thinking his thoughts and understanding his emotions. Again, however, beware of the temptation to get more out of the text than is actually there. Do not devotionalize or spiritualize on the text. Do not try to make striking observations.

Discover the one or two sentences which express the *one central thought or main point* of the ICU. Let the text give its own emphasis, its own main idea. It will be very tempting to impose your own emphasis on the text, depending on how you want to use the text and what point you want it to make. What point, however, did the *writer* intend to stress here? What is the built-in emphasis? Be especially sensitive to *ideas which are repeated* throughout the larger context. Write down the main point and then note the thought-relationship of each sentence to that main point. Keep the entire ICU in mind as you scrutinize each part of it.

Then reread the passage as a whole.

2. *Respace the text,* clause by clause, phrase by phrase. You will find examples of respaced texts in Chapter 8 and in Appendixes A, B, and C. Do not change any of the words or punctuation when you respace the text. The only thing you should change is the spacing of the clauses and phrases. Respacing the text requires two basic mental operations which are at the heart of all

meaningful reading. First you must identify the units of thought (clauses or phrases) in the text. Second, you must identify how each phrase or clause relates to the phrase or clause immediately before it and immediately after it. When you respace the text, you are merely spacing the thought units on the page according to the way they already relate to each other in the text. Usually, the main statements in the ICU should begin at the left margin, and the other phrases, clauses, and sentences should be indented appropriately. Many of the modifying phrases and clauses can begin under the word they modify. Sometimes modifying phrases located within a clause can be respaced above the clause to reveal the uninterrupted flow of thought in that clause. If there are several consecutive thought units which are parallel to each other in thought, space them immediately under each other in order to indicate that parallel relationship. If there is a clause which refers to or explains a certain word in an earlier clause, use a dotted or broken line to indicate that relationship.

You will be better able to spot the structure of each sentence if you take careful note of the connectives and conjunctions (*and, but, for, when, therefore, if, because, after, although, since, so that, till, while,* etc.). You may not be able to respace the text so as to indicate all of the relationships you see, but try to indicate the *basic thought relationships and grammatical relationships* which you find already there in the text.

Then you may want to underline the key words and clauses in your respaced ICU. Reread your respaced text as a whole for meaning. Use this respaced text throughout the rest of your study of this ICU.

Respacing the text is most helpful with didactic portions of Scripture, and may not always be necessary for long narrative portions. If this respacing is done thoughtfully and patiently, several of the following operations will be simplified. The outline will stand out at you. Further relationships will be more easily identified. The condensation will be taken mainly from your underlined sentences.

3. Make a detailed *outline* of the thought progression (the argument) in the ICU. In order to be most informative, each point in your outline, especially the main points, should be a sentence or a long phrase, not merely a word or two. Get your outline from the sense of the text itself. Make your outline as descriptive and interpretive as possible. Avoid cute or alliterated outlines. You may need to experiment with several different outlines before you feel you have the one which fits the text most naturally.

The next chart illustrates a standard outlining system.

After you have outlined the ICU, reread it as a whole for meaning.

4. *Note the function of this ICU* by determining how this ICU relates to the larger context. Why is this ICU included? Why is it included where it is? Note the progression of thought or action in the larger context. Are there any new teachings or new elements in this ICU? How did this ICU function for the original readers? If you tend to think pictorially or graphically, try to diagram the relationships you find between this ICU and the larger context. Then reread the passage as a whole for meaning.

5. *Ask questions of the ICU.* There are six standard questions with which you should begin:

    a. Who? _____ Individuals? Groups? Person speaking? Person spoken to? etc.

    b. When? _____ Chronology? Sequence? What events have just happened? etc.

    c. Where? _____ Geography? (Locate on a map.) Sur-

Traditional Outlining System

I. Ooooo ooooo ooooo ooooo ooooo.
   A. Ooooo ooooo ooooo ooooo.
      1. Ooooo ooooo ooooo.
      2. Ooooo ooooo ooooo.
         a. Ooooo.
         b. Ooooo.
      3. Ooooo ooooo ooooo.
   B. Ooooo ooooo ooooo ooooo.
      1. Ooooo ooooo.
      2. Ooooo ooooo.
II. Ooooo ooooo ooooo ooooo ooooo.
   A. Ooooo ooooo ooooo ooooo.
      1. Ooooo ooooo ooooo.
         a. Ooooo ooooo ooooo
         b. Ooooo ooooo ooooo
            (1) Ooooo
            (2) Ooooo
            (3) Ooooo
         c. Ooooo.
      2. Ooooo ooooo.
         a. Ooooo.
         b. Ooooo.
   B. Ooooo ooooo ooooo.
      1. Ooooo ooooo ooooo ooooo.
      2. Ooooo ooooo ooooo ooooo
         a. Ooooo ooooo
         b. Ooooo ooooo
         c. Ooooo ooooo
   C. Ooooo ooooo ooooo ooooo.
      1. Ooooo ooooo ooooo.
      2. Ooooo ooooo ooooo.
      3. Ooooo ooooo ooooo.

      roundings or setting? etc.
   d. What? _____ Content? Issues? Actions? Events?
      Teachings? Problems? etc.
   e. How? _____ Means? Methods? etc.
   f. Why? _____ Motives? Purpose? Cause? Result? etc.

Then reread the passage as a whole for meaning.

6. *Note grammatical details* such as:

a. The parts of speech (nouns, pronouns, adjectives, verbs, adverbs, prepositions, conjunctions, and interjections)

b. Number (singular or plural)

c. Tense (past perfect, past, present perfect, present, future perfect, future)

d. Voice (active when the subject is acting, or passive when the subject is being acted upon)

e. Mood (indicative when expressing a fact; subjunctive when expressing a possibility or wish; or imperative when expressing a command or request)

f. Antecedents of pronouns

g. Direct objects and indirect objects

Note the overall structural form. Note the particular literary techniques, figures of speech, idioms, employed in this ICU. If you are able, make a grammatical diagram of the key sentences. Then reread the passage as a whole for meaning. (If you are not familiar with the above grammatical details, you should spend some time studying a book on English grammar.)

7. Search out the *internal and external relationships and connections* and *identify them accurately.* Internal relationships are relationships between two or more items *within* this particular ICU. External relationships are relationships between items in this ICU and items in the larger context.

This operation is important for all portions of Scripture, but it is especially crucial for didactic portions. Reflect on each item (each fact, idea, event, etc.) in the ICU and think about how it relates to the rest of the items in the same sentence, in the same ICU, and outside the ICU. Then, when you describe in your notes what you have found, do not merely write that one item "is related to" another item. Instead, describe the actual relationship more accurately by identifying it as one of the relationships listed in the chart on pages 178-79. (Do not be disturbed if you are not immediately able to sort out all of the types of relationships. Nor should you feel that you must memorize technical names for all of these types of relationships. However, the list in the following chart should help you appreciate the fact that there are many types of relationships, and that being aware of the varied types of relationships can help you analyze a Bible passage more thoughtfully and more accurately.) Diagrams and examples of all of these types of relationships are provided in Appendix D.

The point is: Don't just look for isolated facts, ideas, events. Find the connections and relationships that are in the text and describe them as accurately as you can. And do not be satisfied when you have found one or two relationships. Keep looking. After all, *you cannot make inductive inferences unless you first find relationships.* Many of the above relational questions should be asked of the passage in order to identify and clarify the internal and external relationships found in the text.

Sometimes the relationships will be stated explicitly in the text. Other times they will be implicit. The more you ponder the passage, other questions will come to mind as they are stimulated by the events and ideas in the ICU. *Pursue every question.* Some of them will turn out to be very significant avenues of inquiry. The more questions you ask of the passage, the more answers you will discover. Cultivate your curiosity. Ask. Ask. Ask. Remember to write down all of your observations, interpretations, in your notebook. If you tend to think pictorially or graphically, try to diagram the more significant relationships which you find. Then reread the passage as a whole for meaning.

8. *Alter the wording* of the text. Try reading each sentence omitting one word or phrase, then the next, etc., in order to see the contribution which each word or phrase makes to the meaning of the sentence. Do the same with each paragraph, omitting each sentence in turn. Also, it will help you appreciate what the text actually says if you think about what the text could have said but did not. In order to do this, temporarily change each word and each phrase and thus consider a wide variety of substitutions in the text. Try making changes in the grammatical forms of the words (refer to the grammatical details listed in operation 6), as well as changes in the actual words (substituting words which are at times opposite in meaning, and at times close in meaning, to the words which are in the text).

Do not misunderstand the intent of this operation. You are not trying to find wording which makes better sense. If that were your goal, then you would actually be revising the Bible according to your own wisdom. The intent of this operation is not to alter the wording and then leave it in its altered state. The intent is to temporarily alter the wording so that the significance and impact of the "original" wording can be better understood and appreciated. Then reread the passage as a whole for meaning.

If you find that the interpretation of the ICU hinges on the precise meaning of one particular word in the ICU, you may need to do a word study at this point. See chapter 18 for additional thoughts related to word studies.

9. *Paraphrase the ICU* in your own words. Rewrite the entire passage, sentence by sentence. Don't merely look at one word at a time and then substitute a synonym. That can be done with very little thought about the meaning in the ICU. Instead, look at each sentence and think about its meaning in light of the entire ICU. Then

Types of Relationships

One item (one fact, idea, event, etc.) in the text, which will be referred to by using the letter A, could be related to another item, which will be referred to by using the letter B, in a variety of ways. Here are some of the types of relationships that you may find as you examine the text.

1. *Quantitative relationship.* Is A numerically greater than B? Does A occur more often than B? Does A have larger dimensions than B?

2. *Spacial relationship.* How is A located in relation to B? How are A and B located in relation to C?

3. *Chronological relationship* (fixed events). When did A occur? How many days or years separate A and B? What is the order of these fixed events?

4. *Sequential relationship* (order of unfixed events; a set of steps, stages, or events that has a beginning and an end and does not necessarily repeat itself). Does A come before or after B? Is A first, fourth, etc. in the sequence? Is A part of a string of events leading to B?

5. *Cyclical relationship* (a repeating set of steps, stages, forces, events, etc.). Do A and B recur in the same order repeatedly?

6. *Reciprocating or vice versa relationship.* Do A and B occur alternately? Can A lead to B as well as B lead to A? Does A relate to B in the same way that B relates to A?

7. *Cause-effect or parent-offspring relationship.* Does A bring about B? Is A the cause, or one of the causes, of B? Is A the result, or one of the results, of B? Beware of assuming that a chronological or sequential relationship is automatically a cause-effect relationship.

8. *Agency or means-end relationship.* Is A the tool or agent that is used by B to accomplish C?

9. *Comparative or contrastive relationship.* Are A and B identical? Similar? Overlapping? Different? Mutually exclusive? Opposites? Is A positive while B is negative? These relationships can be analyzed by listing the characteristics of A and B in two side-by-side columns and then attempting to match up the character-

istics of A with the characteristics of B.

10. *Supportive relationship.* Is A part of the evidence that supports the proposition B? Is A one of the reasons why B is true?

11. *Inclusive (or the opposite: exclusive) relationship.* Does A (the whole) include B (the part)? Does A exclude B?

12. *Prerequisite relationship.* Must A be true before B can logically be true? Must A take place before B can take place? Is A necessary for B?

13. *Inferential relationship (If-A-then-B).* If A is true, then B will be true. A is sufficient for B.

14. *Value relationship.* Is A more important than B? Is A greater than B?

15. *Authority relationship.* Does A have authority over B? Is B required to submit to A?

16. *Attributional relationship.* Is A one of the attributes, characteristics, or qualities of B? Is A one of the ways in which B functions?

17. *Illustrative relationship.* Is A an example or illustration of B? Is A "applied" to (or explained in terms of) B so as to clarify A?

18. *Evaluative relationship.* Does A give the worth of, or describe the value of, B?

19. *Problem-solution or question-answer relationship.* Is A the problem to which B is the solution? Is A the question that is answered by B?

20. *Principle-application relationship.* Is A the moral principle while B describes the practical application of A?

21. *Secondary or sibling relationship.* Are A and B parts of the same whole? Results of the same cause? Are A and B related to each other only because they are primarily related to C?

22. *Unrelated.* Are A and B completely independent of each other? Totally irrelevant to each other?

Of course, the types of relationships listed above often overlap. Also, you may often find that A and B are related to each other in more than one way.

substitute another sentence which is made up of mostly different words but which means exactly the same thing. Then reread the passage as a whole for meaning.

10. *List the main teachings* which are stated explicitly or implicitly in the ICU. An explicit teaching is one that is stated clearly and directly in the text. Explicit teachings are easy to list. However, *be very careful when listing implicit teachings.* Implicit teachings include (1) ideas which must be assumed in order for the explicit statements in the passage to make sense, or (2) ideas which can be inferred from the explicit statements in the passages. For example, Genesis 1:1 does not explicitly state that God exists. Nevertheless, that verse cannot make sense unless it is assumed that God does in fact exist. Thus, the idea that God exists would be an implicit teaching of Genesis 1:1. The idea that God created the heavens and the earth would be an explicit teaching of Genesis 1:1.

Then reread the passage as a whole for meaning.

11. *Write a condensation* of the ICU. Boil down the essence of the text into a summary which is approximately one-fifth as long as the ICU. Be sure to include all the essential events and ideas contained in the ICU, only in abbreviated form. Then reread the passage as a whole for meaning.

12. Write a *quiz* based on this ICU made up of true-false, fill-in-the-blank, and short-answer questions. Or, if the ICU is a narrative, write a brief *report* (a front-page article, or a magazine special) describing the events and the persons involved. Or, *draw* a picture of the setting. Or, write a *diary* entry which records the events and feelings from one or several individuals' points of view. Then reread the passage as a whole for meaning.

Each of these twelve operations requires a different mental process. It is important not only that each of the twelve operations be complete, but also that they be completed in the order in which they are listed.

When you have completed all of the operations with this ICU, do the same with the next ICU, etc.

Occasionally review your titles for the major divisions, subdivisions, and ICUs so that you can keep an overview of the entire book fresh in your mind.

Step 5—Examine Topics

Study topics throughout the book. For example, what does the book say about the Scriptures, God, Jesus, the Holy Spirit, Satan, man, sin, faith, salvation, righteous living, the church, the future, etc.? You may also want to choose topics about which you have written interesting observations or questions. Also study key words used repeatedly in the book, especially words which you suspect might be used in a special technical sense. Along with regular topics and key words, you might find it interesting to trace various categories of statements, such as commands, warnings, etc. through the book. Be sure to note to whom these are addressed, conditions placed on the promises, etc.

As you examine everything that the book has to say on whatever topics and key words you choose, you will not want to be content merely to tabulate all the statements. Also ponder them, relate them, and summarize them. Be sure to study each topic in light of (1) how it relates to the main thrust of the book, and (2) how each mention of the topic relates to the ICU in which it is found.

More specific procedures for studying a topic throughout the entire Bible are spelled out in chapter 18.

Step 6—Synthesize

Put all the parts together (all the ICUs, subdivisions, and topics). Relate all the parts to each other. Integrate all the parts into a meaningful whole. As you do so, you may need to revise some of your initial survey findings, your major divisions, etc.

Combine your titles and think through the entire book. You may even want to memorize your main titles. Also combine your outlines of each ICU so that you have a complete outline of the book. Combine your condensations of each ICU so that you have a running summary of the whole book.

Reread the entire book. Write a brief capsule (three or four sentences) which expresses the heart of the book.

Step 7—Compare

Up to this point you should have used interpretive aids sparingly. Now, however, you should compare your understanding of the book with the understandings of others by using a variety of interpretive aids. When you find differences of interpretation, carefully examine the reasons they give for their interpretations. Then reexamine the reasons for your own interpretation. Remember that the Bible book itself is your final appeal. Any "debate" should drive you back to the Bible.

Also compare your findings with what you have already discovered in your study of other Bible books and topics. Relate and integrate.

Step 8—Apply

Put the teachings you have discovered to use in your life. Of course, any applications which can be made before this step are commended, provided you are certain you have the proper interpretation before you make the application. Go back and read through all the practical applications you thought of while you were writing out your observations and interpretations. Some of the principles may find direct application in your life. In other cases you may have to discern the general spiritual principle underlying the various specific statements and situations, so that principle be can be transferred to your circumstances. Consider all possibilities. Are there some passages you should memorize, some commands you should obey, some examples to follow, some promises to claim, some errors to avoid, some attitudes to adopt?

Finally, do not neglect to share your findings with others.

18

The Procedure for Studying Topics

Whether your topic or subject is a doctrine, an aspect of Christian living, a biographical study, or any other type of topic, do not be satisfied merely to look up the topic in one of the interpretive aids. Naturally, you will want to find out what others say about the topic later, but for now you want to go directly to the Bible.

Topical study in the Bible requires that you make a conscious effort to be open-minded and objective. Instead of coming to the Bible in order to prove your point, come expecting to discover. Form the habit of reserving final conclusions until all the evidence is in. Also beware of the fallacy of determining your beliefs on the basis of your experience. Learn to evaluate your experience in the light of the Bible, not vice versa.

The eight steps in the procedure for studying topics in the Bible are:

1. Pray
2. Delimit
3. Recall
4. Find and Sort
5. Scrutinize
6. Synthesize
7. Compare
8. Apply

Step 1—Pray

See Step 1 in chapter 17.

Step 2—Delimit

The word *delimit* means to narrow down your general topic. First, state your general topic. Then write out all the specific questions you can think of which pertain to that topic. Then identify those questions which are basic or foundational. These are the questions which must be answered first, in order for the other questions to be answered. Concentrate your study on these basic questions. You will be able to answer the other questions relatively easily after you have settled the basic issues. Many topical studies go astray because the fundamental questions are not answered first.

Step 3—Recall

Search your own mind. Write out your present assumptions, definitions, concepts, and ideas on this topic. Be careful not to extend your present assumptions and ideas into the Bible as you study this topic. By recalling your present assumptions and ideas on the topic and thus identifying the mental "baggage" which you bring to the study, you will be able to be more objective during your study and to let the Bible speak for itself. After you have completed your study of the topic you can evaluate your initial assumptions and ideas.

Step 4—Find and Sort

Obtain the references for all the passages which are relevant to your topic. Begin by searching your memory for Bible passages which mention, discuss, or illustrate the topic. Then find more references by using your large concordance. In order to use your concordance you will need to have a list of key words to use in finding the references. Refer to what you wrote out under step 2 and list all the key words used there, along with synonyms for those key words. Then systematically search your large concordance using the key words and synonyms to obtain all the references where each of those words is used.

Finding all the verses which use a certain English word is easy. Merely look up that word in the main body of your concordance and all the references are listed for you. However, if you stop there your study will not be as accurate or as complete as it could be. By using a large concordance such as *Young's* or *Strong's* (which, you will recall, are based on the wording of the King James Version) or the *New American Standard Exhaustive Concordance* you can find out much more. Keep in mind that translation is not a simple mechanical process of taking each Greek word and substituting an equivalent English word. This means that a Greek word which is translated into one particular English word in one passage may be translated into a different English word in another passage. It also means that an English word which represents one particular Greek word in one passage may represent a different Greek word in another passage. For instance, the word *servant* in the New Testament of the King James Version represents several Greek words, including *diakonos, doulos,* and *pais,* each of which has a slightly different literal definition. Thus, if you are studying about servants, it might help you interpret each passage more accurately if you are aware of these various Greek words and their various literal definitions. Your large concordance will give you the various Greek words represented by any given English word along with their literal definitions. But your study is not complete yet, because each of the Greek words which is translated *servant* may be translated into other English words in other passages. For example, *diakonos* is sometimes translated "minister" and sometimes "deacon." The various English words which were used to translate each given Greek word are listed at the back of the concordance. With these additional English words, more verses can be found by looking up each additional English word in the main body of the concordance. A full set of instructions on how to use your concordance can be found in the concordance's preface or introduction.

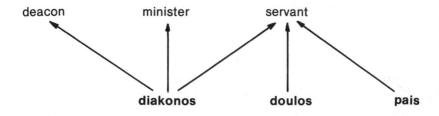

Your study of words and topics will always be more accurate and complete if you focus your attention on the Greek and Hebrew words rather than merely on the English words.

As you are doing this research in your concordance, take careful note of the literal definitions of each Greek or Hebrew word, and of the differences between the definitions of the various words which are translated into the same English word. Keep in mind, however, that a word is defined ultimately by its usage in a particular context; thus the literal meaning given in the concordance cannot always be forced onto the word as it appears in the various contexts where you find it. Of course, the current (at the time of writing), commonly accepted literal understanding of the word should be your starting point in interpreting its meaning in any given passage.

But beware of becoming overly mechanical in your attention to words. Remember that the same word is often used to refer to different concepts. For example, compare the apostle John's use of the word *world* (Greek: *kosmos*) in John 3:16 with his use of the same word in 1 John 2:15. Also remember that different words are often used to refer to the same concept.

You can also find additional passages by using a topical Bible such as *Nave's Topical Bible*, or a concordance which lists words used in several modern translations such as *The Zondervan Expanded Concordance*. The main difference between a concordance and a topical Bible is that a concordance merely lists the verses which use a certain word, whereas a topical Bible lists passages which include a certain *idea* or *concept*, even though the word for that idea or concept may not appear in the passage. When you use a topical Bible, you must not assume just because a passage is listed under a certain topic that the passage is actually talking about that topic. That is for you to determine.

After you have found all the passages that are relevant to your topic, you must sort them. As you come to each reference, look up the passage and read it in its context. Then classify it by writing down the reference under one of the following four headings:

Category 1: Definitive-long passages.—This category includes passages which meet all four of the following requirements:

a. definitely and directly on the subject at hand (more than merely related to the subject by inference);

b. only one likely interpretation;

c. not figurative; and

d. extended (several sentences rather than merely an incidental reference to the subject at hand).

Category 2: Definitive-short passages.—These passages meet the same requirements as above except that they are brief, often just one sentence.

Category 3: Inferential passages.—These passages imply something about the subject at hand. They *indirectly* say something about your topic.

Category 4: Vague passages.—Such passages have two or more possible interpretations. Many figurative passages belong in this category.

Beware of the temptation of placing passages into category 1 or category 2 merely because they appear to favor the viewpoint you were hoping to find. Be as objective as possible in your sorting. This, of course, is an initial categorization; you may want to reclassify many of the passages as you study them more in depth. Keep a careful record in your notebook of all the references which belong in each category. You may find it helpful to keep your list of references under each category in Bible-book-order.

Step 5—Scrutinize

Scrutinize, analyze, examine, meditate on each passage. Make a thorough study of each passage in turn, beginning with category 1. Give special attention to the *context* of each passage. Note the single main point that is being made in the immediate context. There is a great temptation, especially in topical study, to study passages only in the light of the other parallel passages or related passages, so that the other passages become the context. However, each passage must be examined primarily in the light of *its own* context. Compare passage with passage only after you have compared each passage with its own context.

Furthermore, be careful to keep in mind the fact that revelation progressed gradually throughout Bible his-

tory, and each passage must be understood in the context of its proper dispensation.

In studying each passage in its own context, especially in studying the first two categories of passages, it
would be wise to adopt a procedure similar to step 4 of
the procedure for studying books in chapter 17, including
the following:

a. Carefully *read the passage and its context for
meaning.* Read it several times, sometimes in different
translations for comparison. Do not read meaning into
the passage. What is the *one main point* being made in
this context? Find the sentence which best expresses
the main point of the immediate context and then note
how the other sentences relate to this key sentence.
This will help you identify how this passage functions
in relation to its context.

b. Respace the text.

c. Outline the passage.

d. Ask six standard questions (who? when? where?
what? how? why?).

e. Note grammatical details.

f. Identify relationships.

g. Alter the wording.

h. Paraphrase the passage.

i. Condense the passage.

Sometimes the passage you are studying becomes a
puzzle because its interpretation hinges on the precise
meaning of one particular word in the passage. You will
need to do a word study before you can complete your
study of that passage. There are some principles regarding word studies which are important to keep in
mind. You will remember that each word is usually defined by its immediate context. But, when the context

allows the word to have several meanings, or several shades of meaning, and each of those several meanings makes sense in that passage, another factor other than the context becomes increasingly important in determining the precise meaning that the word has in that passage. It is the current (at the time of writing) usage of a word that supplies the starting point for understanding a word in any given passage. Since the word's current usage is always the starting point, you will need to find out how that word is used in its entire Testament. In other words, with the help of your large concordance find out how that particular Greek word is used throughout the New Testament or how that particular Hebrew word is used throughout the Old Testament, even in passages which do not directly relate to your topic. It is especially helpful to find out how the author of the passage you are puzzled about uses that particular word elsewhere in the same book or in other books. If you find that the word has a wide variety of meanings in the other passages where it is used, then you will not be able to dogmatically adopt any of those meanings for the word in your puzzling passage. However, if you find that the word is consistently used to mean just one thing in those other passages, then you have good reason to adopt that one meaning for the word in your puzzling passage. Of course, the fewer times a word is used in its Testament, the less valid this process becomes.

Word studies (including the studies of the etymologies of words) are intentionally deemphasized in this guidebook. An overemphasis on word studies often comes from a basic misconception about the nature of language. Meanings do not adhere in words, but in human beings. Thus, the really significant question is not "What does this *word* mean?" but "What does this biblical *writer* mean when he uses this word?" Now, of course, certain words are customarily used to express certain meanings, and dictionaries tell us what those customary meanings are. Also, an awareness of the lexical (dictionary) definition of a particular word is a necessary element in the process of interpretation. Nevertheless, no writer is limited to customary usage when he expresses his thoughts. Thought is bigger than language. Words are the servants of the writer or speaker; they are not his master. Words are the flexible raw materials of the craftsman, but as with any other expressive art, the whole is greater than the sum of its parts. Although a *tentative* meaning of a word can be gained from a study of that word *in isolation,* a full grasp of the meaning of that word *in a given passage* must go beyond the lexicon to an examination of the word *in context.* Similarly, although a rudimentary idea of the meaning of a passage can be gained from the study of the various words in isolation, a proper grasp of the meaning of that passage must go beyond isolated words to an examination of the passage as a whole.

What can an overemphasis on word studies lead to? Some people build their theology, not on a study of what the biblical writers say, but on what the lexicons and etymological reference works say about isolated terms. Thus, they pay more attention to word-definitions-in-isolation than to words-in-relation-to-other-words in context. They pay more attention to etymologies (the flow of historical usage of a word) than to the flow of the argument of the biblical writer. This procedure violates the nature of language and results in a theology which reflects the lexicon more than it reflects the Bible. Thus, word studies should never be an end in themselves. Nor should they be the starting point of one's study of theology. In fact, as far as Bible interpretation is concerned, word studies have no reason for existence in themselves; they are legitimate only when they are incorporated as part of a study of a passage, as explained above.

When you are studying several passages on a given topic, remember to interpret the less clear passages (inferential and vague passages) in light of the clear ones. As you study each passage in turn, you will probably reclassify many of your passages into different categories. In fact, you may decide after thorough examination that some passages do not belong in any of the four categories. You may discover that some passages which appeared to be relevant to the topic at first reading actually bear no relationship at all to the topic. Preserve your notes on these passages, however, especially if you suspect that others might build a case for their viewpoint on any of these irrelevant passages. Sometimes it is just as important to know why a passage does not settle an issue as it is to know what a passage does say about the issue.

Do not limit your thinking to the traditional structure or "sides" of the problem, especially with debatable topics. Ask new questions. Look for unexplored ways of putting the evidence together. For example, do not confine your possible solutions to merely dichotomy or trichotomy, merely Calvinism or Arminianism, etc. Search for other ways of organizing your ideas.

After you have come this far in your study of your topic, you may find that you need to lay a better foundation for yourself by setting the study aside for a while in order to study some other area which is basic to your study. For example, after studying about Satan, you may realize that you should also study the subject of angels in general before you draw your conclusions. Or, after studying the topic of tongues, you may realize that you should also study the baptism and filling of the Holy Spirit before you draw your conclusions.

Step 6—Synthesize

Put it all together. After you have studied through all the passages in each category, review all of your research, especially your findings from the passages which end up in the first two categories. Your conclusions should not be based on vague passages. Write out your conclusions in a carefully worded statement in your own words. Constantly ask yourself, (1) Are my interpretations and conclusions based on good evidence in Scripture? (2) Have I examined all of the evidence which is relevant to this topic? and (3) Have I considered all the alternative interpretations?

Then write out the questions which still puzzle you, the issues which are still unresolved in your thinking. Also think through the implications your findings have for other related areas of doctrine, Christian living, etc.

Step 7—Compare

Up to this point you should have used interpretive aids sparingly. Now, however, you should compare your understandings of the topic with the understandings of others by using a variety of interpretive aids. When you find different interpretations and conclusions, examine carefully the reasons they give for their interpretations and conclusions. Then reexamine the reasons for your own. Remember that the Bible is the final authority on this topic.

Also compare your findings with what you have already discovered in your study of other Bible books and topics. Relate and integrate.

Step 8—Apply

Put the teachings you have discovered to use in your life and share your findings with others.

19

Summary:
Thirty Key Principles of Bible Study

The most basic and most important ideas which are discussed in the preceding chapters are here condensed into thirty key principles.

1. Respect the Bible as God's inspired, reliable Word. Approach it prayerfully and with an open mind, ready to respond by obedience whenever appropriate. Beware of Bible study done out of a motive of pride or self-enhancement.

2. The Holy Spirit will teach you as you actively engage in the work of Bible study with his help.

3. Go *directly* to the Bible instead of depending on sources about the Bible (interpretive aids).

4. *Discover* what the Bible says. Let the Bible speak for itself by using an inductive process, rather than reading meaning into the text.

5. Keep these three phases in their proper logical order: first observe; then interpret; then apply.

6. During each step and operation of Bible study, keep the distinction between observation and interpretation clearly in mind. Interpretation of what the text *means* must be based on systematic observation of what the text *says*, not on assumptions which you bring to the text.

7. Do not overlook the clear, straightforward statements of the passage.

8. Seek to understand each passage as the writer and original readers understood it.

9. Learn as much Greek and Hebrew as you can, but do not substitute that knowledge for proper hermeneutics and thorough Bible study procedure.

10. Remember that each passage has only one correct interpretation, which may have many applications.

11. Use *literary* interpretation. Begin with a literal understanding of the passage, and then make whatever adjustments are called for by the figurative elements in the passage, determined in light of the context.

12. Interpret each passage according to its historical and cultural background.

13. Always examine a passage's *context* carefully, especially its immediate context. Interpret every passage in light of its context.

14. Do not let an overemphasis on details or mechanical procedures hide the message of the text. Read and study each passage as a whole for meaning.

15. When studying a topic, examine *all* the passages which are relevant to the topic.

16. Compare passage with passage. Interpret less clear passages in light of clear ones.

17. Use such noninterpretive aids as an English dictionary, a set of Bible maps, and a large concordance throughout your study procedure.

18. After you have arrived at your own interpretations and conclusions, carefully examine what others say by using a variety of interpretive aids.

19. Reason properly. Avoid circular reasoning based on unfounded assumptions, overgeneralizing, arguing from silence, arguing by analogy, and misusing the converse and inverse.

20. Persevere and be patient. Keep examining the text, and keep asking (1) Do I have all the relevant facts?

and (2) Have I considered various possible interpretations?

21. Be willing to proceed slowly and suspend judgment on difficult matters when necessary. Distinguish between primary and secondary matters.

22. No translation is perfect. Use one or two translations as your basic study Bibles, but also keep a few other translations handy for survey readings and for comparisons, passage by passage.

23. Your basic study Bible(s) should be an accurate translation, relatively literal rather than a paraphrase. It should also use current English and should be a committee translation.

24. Read through the Bible to get a bird's-eye view before you begin intensive study of a book or topic.

25. Generally, book study should precede topic study, since book study lays a necessary foundation for topic study.

26. The Bible's teachings are not merely to be understood, they are to be applied in our lives. However, application must be based on correct interpretation. General spiritual principles can be applied directly; specific examples and commands must be examined in order to uncover the underlying general spiritual principle which can then be applied.

27. Write out your thoughts. Organize your notes in a loose-leaf notebook rather than marking up your Bible.

28. Adopt a procedure for studying Bible books which follows the whole-parts-whole pattern, namely: (1) pray; (2) survey the book; (3) divide the book into its natural divisions; (4) scrutinize each unit of immediate context in succession; (5) examine topics throughout the book; (6) synthesize the parts into a meaningful whole; (7) compare your findings with the findings of others; and (8) apply your findings in your life.

29. Scrutinize each successive unit of immediate context using a variety of operations, namely: (1) read the unit for meaning; (2) respace the text; (3) outline the unit; (4) note the function of the unit in its larger context; (5) ask six standard questions of the unit; (6) note grammatical details in the unit; (7) identify internal and external relationships; (8) temporarily alter the wording; (9) paraphrase the unit; (10) list the unit's main teachings; (11) condense the unit; and (12) employ other operations which fit the nature of the unit.

30. Adopt a thorough procedure for studying Bible topics, namely: (1) pray; (2) delimit the topic; (3) recall your present ideas on the topic; (4) find all the passages relevant to the topic and sort them into appropriate categories; (5) scrutinize each passage; (6) synthesize your findings from the definitive passages; (7) compare your findings with the findings of others; and (8) apply your findings in your life.

Appendix A

Sample Results from a Book Study

The book chosen for this study is the Book of Philippians. You should not read this appendix until after you begin your own study of Philippians. This appendix is not designed to present a full study of the book; rather, it merely illustrates various parts of the study procedure. Thus, only selected portions from only five of the eight steps in the procedure are included. If you merely read this appendix without doing your own study of Philippians, you will receive a distorted picture of the correct book study procedure. You will profit much more if you carefully work through each step given in chapter 17 on your own. Then, after you complete each step, refer to this appendix and compare your results with whatever results are included here.

It is not important that your results be identical to the results given here. It *is* important, however, that you do your own work by carefully following the procedures given in chapter 17.

Step 1—Pray

Step 2—Survey

The first survey readings of Philippians leave several general impressions, such as: (1) the book is actually a personal letter which focuses often on the author's close relationship with the Philippians; (2) the book repeatedly mentions continuance and growth in the Christian life; (3) the book seems to be very positive, mentioning joy many times, etc.

Additional survey readings indicate the following:

1. Writer, origin, and date. The first verse in the book reveals that it was from both Paul and Timothy. However, the first person singular pronoun (I, me, my) is used throughout the letter, and Timothy is discussed in the third person (he, him, his) in 2:19-23. Thus, it can be inferred that Paul was the one who was most directly responsible for the content of the letter (under inspiration, of course). It is clear that Paul was writing from prison (1:7,13,16-19), perhaps in Rome (1:13; 4:22). The Book of Philippians itself does not give the precise date of writing. It would be necessary to study Acts and other historical sources in order to determine the dates of Paul's Roman imprisonments.

2. Recipients and destination. The recipients were "all the saints . . . including the overseers and deacons" (1:1), although one portion is addressed to an individual, the "true comrade" (4:3). The place of destination is the city of Philippi (1:1; 4:15), and this letter *may* have been carried to the Philippians by Epaphroditus (compare 2:25 with 2:19).

3. Date of events. None of the events mentioned in the letter are clearly linked with any key historical events.

4. Occasion and purpose. Paul's previous experiences in Philippi are found easily by looking up "Philippi" in a concordance. Acts 16 supplies the main narrative. At the time of writing, Paul was in prison and had recently received a gift which Epaphroditus brought from the Philippians (4:10-19; 2:25). Paul did not expressly state any singular purpose for writing. However, the content of the letter suggests that he probably wrote in order to express his appreciation for their gift, to encourage them personally in their spiritual lives, and to exhort them regarding unity and false righteousness.

5. Literature. The Book of Philippians is a letter—a very personal letter. Paul's feelings are stated quite frequently throughout the letter, and they are mostly positive—although there are occasional references to negative feelings.

6. Main thrusts. Paul does not explicitly label any particular idea as his basic message or central theme. However, he does include extended sections on the subjects of unity and false righteousness. Also, he encourages the Philippians throughout the letter, repeatedly emphasizing continued growth and the advance of the gospel.

7. See Step 3 below.

It is helpful at this point to find out more about the city of Philippi. The book of Philippians itself does not give any information about Philippi. However, several facts about the city and its people are found by looking up all the other references to Philippi in the New Testament, especially Acts 16. Also, a number of helpful additional facts about Philippi and its inhabitants are discovered by reading about the city in Bible dictionaries and Bible encyclopedias.

Step 3—Divide

Longer books of the Bible might have major divisions, subdivisions, and ICUs. Philippians, however, divides most naturally into just seven ICUs. Also, in contrast to many other Bible books, this personal letter has no single, unique, overriding theme (no theme around which the entire letter is organized and no theme which is not also contained in the other letters in the New Testament). Thus, no attempt is made to force a theme onto the book by giving an arbitrary title to the seven ICUs. See the chart of Philippians which follows.

It is frequently said that the theme of Philippians is joy. While it is true that Paul mentions joy many times, joy is certainly not the organizing theme of the letter. There are no extended sections dealing expressly with the subject of joy. Also, each mention of joy is incidental to the subject being discussed in the ICU, rather than being a mention of joy for the purpose of discussing joy itself.

Step 4—Scrutinize

Rather than attempting to illustrate the direct results from all twelve of the operations described in chapter 17, only the respaced text, outline, paraphrase, and condensation of Philippians 1:3-11 are given here. Then selected observations-interpretations-applications are given in order to illustrate the use of the form shown in chapter 17. Of course, such observations are made as you carry out the twelve operations, and different people might make the same observations while carrying out different operations.

Philippians 1:3-11 Respaced:

3 I thank my God
        in all my remembrance of you,
4   always offering prayer
                with joy in my every prayer for you all,
5   in view of your participation in the gospel
                        from the first day
                        until now.
6   For I am confident of this very thing,
                that He who began a good work in you

```
                          will perfect it
                             until the day of Christ Jesus.
7            For it is only right for me to feel this way about you all,
                          because I have you in my heart,
                    since      both in my imprisonment
                               and in the defense and confirmation of
                          \      the gospel,
                          you all are partakers of grace with me.
8            For God is my witness,
                          how I long for you all
                               with the affection of Christ Jesus.
9     And this I pray,
                 that your love may abound
                               still more and more
                               in real knowledge and all discernment,
10                   so that you may approve the things that are excellent,
                               in order to be sincere and blameless
                                     until the day of Christ;
11           having been filled with the fruit of righteousness
                                which comes through Jesus Christ,
                          to the glory and praise of God. (Author's
                          underlines)
```

Philippians 1:13-11 Outlined

I. (ICU title) Affection and Prayer (1:3-11)
   A. Paul's personal, affectionate relationship with the Philippians (3-8)
      1. His thankfulness and joy because of the Philippians' help (3-5)
      2. His confidence regarding God's continuing work in the Philippians (6)
      3. His underlying affection and common bond with the Philippians (7-8)
   B. Paul's prayer for the Philippians' spiritual growth (9-11)

The Book of Philippians

1:1-2 Greeting

1:3-11 Affection and Prayer

1:12-26 Imprisonment for Christ

1:27 to 2:18 Exhortations regarding Oneness and Witness

2:19-30 Sending Timothy and Epaphroditus

3:1 to 4:1 Beware False Righteousness

4:2-9 Miscellaneous Exhortations

4:10-20 Your Gift

4:21-23 Close

Philippians 1:3-11 Paraphrased

[3]Whenever I remember you Philippians, I always thank God [4]and always pray with real happiness [5]because you have always been faithful in sharing in the spread of the gospel. [6]I am sure that God will not stop working in you now, but will continue working until the day of Christ Jesus. [7]I have good reason to feel this way because of the personal bond we have as corecipients of God's grace—in my imprisonment as well as in explaining and proving the gospel. [8]God knows how deeply I care for all of you, a feeling prompted by Jesus Christ. [9]I pray for your love to expand with more and more insight [10]in order for you to properly evaluate the true character and value of things. Then you will be able to be pure and upright until the day of Christ, [11]having a life which grows out of our righteousness from Jesus Christ, and which magnifies God.

Philippians 1:3-11 Condensed

Beloved Philippians, I joyfully thank God because of your participation in the gospel, assured (by our mutual experience of God's grace) that God will continue working in you. I pray for your continuing growth in spiritual insight and righteous living.

Reference Philippians 1:3-11 **Title** Affection and Prayer **Page** ____

(translation ____ N.A.S.B. ____ **)** **Date** ____

Verses	Observations	Resultant Interpretations and Questions	Practical Applications
3	1. Paul thanks God, not the Philippians.	(Based on obs. 2, 3, and 4) Paul feels a close, personal affection for, and a mutual bond, not with merely a few select Philippian believers, but with *all* of them. No doubt this includes Euodia and Syntyche, two women who needed correction (see 4:2).	We should not interact only with those in our select clique. Rather, we should identify with all believers and express our affection for all believers.
4,7,7,8 (see also v. 1)	2. Repeatedly says "you all"		
4,7,8	3. This ICU contains 3 statements of emotion, all of which are positive affections ("joy," "I have you in my heart," and "I long for you all with the affection of Christ Jesus"). Furthermore, each statement of affection is grammatically linked with a "you all."		
5,7	4. Mutual sharing between Paul and the Philippians is mentioned twice ("your participation in the gospel," and "partakers of grace with me"). Again, both are grammatically linked with a "you all."		
3-4	5. When Paul remembers the Philippians he is always thankful; when he prays for them he is always joyful.	(Based on obs. 5 and 6) A thankful and joyful spirit could easily be present without it necessarily showing up in the wording of the prayer; so verses 3-4 may refer to the spirit rather than the actual wording of Paul's prayers for the Philippians. — OR — Perhaps Paul does in fact express thankfulness and joy whenever he prays for them, but his "sample" prayer in verses 9-11 represents only part of his complete prayers for the Philippians.	Our prayers for other believers should be thankful and joyful, *and* we should pray for their spiritual growth.
9-11	6. (Compare obs. 5) Paul's prayer for the Philippians' spiritual growth in verses 9-11 is neither thankful nor joyful (at least not *explicitly* so).		
3,6,8,11 6,8,10,11	7. "God" (and "He") is mentioned four times, and "Christ" is mentioned four times.	Does "God" always mean just "God our Father" or does "God" include all three	

Ref	Observation	Question / Interpretation	Application
6,9	However, there is no mention of the Holy Spirit in this ICU. (The same absence exists in 1:1-2.)	members of the trinity? Why is the Holy Spirit not mentioned in this ICU? Why is he mentioned so infrequently in the entire letter?	
	8. The Philippians are spoken of as changing and improving over time. "He who began ... will perfect it," "that your love may abound still more and more" (compare 1:25).	Christian maturity appears to be something believers grow toward gradually, rather than something they can arrive at instantaneously.	Beware of easy formulas promising quick maturity.
6,10	9. The phrase "until the day of Christ" appears twice, first in connection with God perfecting his work and second in connection with the Philippians' sincerity and blamelessness (compare 2:16).	What, and when, is the day of Christ? —perhaps a day of judgment (?) —perhaps at the return of Christ (?) —perhaps it relates to 3:20-21 (?)	
6,9-10	10. The Philippians' growth is spoken of as both God's doing and their doing. "He who began ... will perfect it." "Your love ... so that you may approve" (compare 2:12-13).	Christian growth involves *both* God's action and my action.	We cannot expect to grow if we are passive. We must faithfully carry out our responsibilities.
6,11	11. Singular: "good work" (not "works"), and "fruit of righteousness" (not "fruits") (compare Galatians 5:22).		
6	12. Note the wording of verse 6. Paul is "confident" (not merely "hopeful") that "He" (God) (not "the Philippians") would perfect what was started.	Would Paul also have been *confident* that the *Philippians* would continue? If God perfects his work in the Philippians, can they do anything but continue? (Was it impossible for the Philippians to stop growing or to "backslide"?) —perhaps this was possible, but God would faithfully continue doing his part anyhow (?)	
9-11	13. Note the prerequisite relationships established by the words "so that" and "in order."	(Based on obs. 13 and 14) Love and knowledge are vitally linked in these verses. Knowledge is basic to proper values (approving the things that are excellent) and to a life that is sincere and blameless. Yet, knowledge is not an end in itself, for Paul prays for their love to increase.	We should seek all the knowledge and discernment we can get, but our reason should be in order to enlarge our love.
9	14. Paul prays that their "love may abound still more and more" (not merely that their knowledge may abound).		

Notice that some observations do not have written interpretations. Notice also that no applications are stated when the interpretation column contains a question or is uncertain.

Step 5—Examine Topics

There are many topics which deserve your close attention in the Book of Philippians. One which Paul speaks about repeatedly is the subject of *unity and disunity.* In fact, this subject comes very close to being a theme for the book. It is especially important, when studying the topic of unity and disunity in Philippians to examine how each mention of the topic relates to the developing thought in the immediate context.

Step 6—Synthesize

The following four-sentence capsule summarizes the heart of the book of Philippians:

Paul, to the Philippian Christians:

Dear brothers and sisters in the Lord, I love and rejoice in you and in your repeated generosity, and I pray for you constantly. My imprisonment has actually advanced the gospel, yet I hope to be released and see you soon (in the meantime I am sending Epaphroditus and Timothy). I exhort you to live and witness in united harmony as you view each other with Jesus' humble, servant attitude. Remember to place your trust for righteousness only in the Lord Jesus, and also keep growing in, living for, and rejoicing in him.

Step 7—Compare

_____

Step 8—Apply

_____

Appendix B

Sample Results from a Topic Study

The topic chosen for this study is *the content of the gospel message.* You should not read this appendix until after you begin your own study of this topic. This appendix is not designed to present a full study of the topic; rather, it merely illustrates various parts of the study procedure. Thus, only selected portions from only five of the eight steps in the procedure are included. If you merely read this appendix without doing your own study of the topic, you will receive a distorted picture of the correct procedure. You will profit much more if you carefully work through each step given in chapter 18 on your own. Then, after you complete each step, refer to this appendix and compare your results with whatever results are included here.

It is not important that your results be identical to the results given here. It *is* important, however, that you do your own work by carefully following the procedure given in chapter 18.

Step 1—Pray

_____

Step 2—Delimit

The general topic is the content of the gospel message (the plan of salvation).

Some of the specific questions which pertain to this topic are:

1. What exactly does the word *gospel* mean?

2. What facts make up the content of the gospel message? Or, what facts must a person understand and consider true before he can respond to the gospel?

3. Is there one verse in the Bible which contains the entire gospel message, and thus can be considered the gospel in a nutshell?

4. What was the content of the gospel messages which Jesus preached? Which the apostles preached?

5. Are there different gospel messages? Is there a separate message for Old Testament times? for the Jews? for Gentiles? for children? for people with different problems?

6. What are the contents of the false gospels mentioned in the New Testament?

7. What response is the proper response to the gospel?

8. Should good works or anything else be added to one's response to the gospel?

9. What is the proper means through which the gospel message should be communicated? Are there a variety of means which are acceptable?

10. Is the evangelist's responsibility merely to explain the gospel message, or is his responsibility also to persuade the hearer to respond positively?

11. Is it possible to understand or accept only part of the gospel message and still be saved?

12. Can everyone understand the gospel message? How old must a person be before he can understand it?

13. Has everyone who has ever lived heard the gospel message? If not, is there a different plan of salvation for those who have not heard the gospel?

If you were to attempt to answer all of these questions in one comprehensive study, you would probably become frustrated. Thus, two questions are selected which appear to be basic to the rest of the questions:

1. What exactly does the word *gospel* mean?
2. What facts make up the content of the gospel message? Or, what facts must a person understand and consider true before he can respond to the gospel?

This present study concentrates strictly on these two questions. You should temporarily set aside the rest of the questions until you have satisfactorily answered these foundational questions.

Step 3—Recall

Each person's prior ideas will be different. It is not important that you know what someone else's prior ideas were. But it *is* important that you identify your own mental "baggage" before you proceed further with your study.

Step 4—Find and Sort

After listing a few references from memory, many additional references are found by looking up key words in a large concordance. The key words in the two basic questions which were selected in step 2 are *gospel, message,* and *content.*

The word *content* is not used in the King James Version in the same sense in which it is being used here. Thus, *content* does not lead to any references. The words *message* and *messenger* (both from *epaggelia*), and the word *promise* (also from *epaggelia*) are also of little help. For example, *message* does lead to 1 John 1:5 and 3:11, which appear at first glance to be relevant verses. However, a reading of the context of these verses shows that they refer to a message for people who are already saved, rather than the gospel message (the plan of salvation) for people who are still unsaved. Thus, *message* and its related words do not lead to any

relevant passages either. It would be a mistake, however, to think that the time spent searching for references by using the words *content* and *message* is
wasted time. In your efforts to locate every relevant passage, you will often follow leads which go nowhere.
However, you should still follow every possible lead in
locating references. Only by such a thorough search can
you be sure that your subsequent study and conclusions
are based on all that the Bible says about the topic.

It turns out that this particular study revolves around
just one key word, the word *gospel*. Also, no English
synonyms for *gospel* are used. Any selecting of synonyms would have to be based on an assumption regarding the exact meaning of the word *gospel*. Such an assumption should not be allowed to enter into the study,
especially since one of the two basic questions in this
particular study has to do with the exact meaning of the
word *gospel*.

The fact that this study revolves around just one English word without synonyms should not be taken as typical of most topic studies. Often, there will be several key
words from the basic questions, each of which will lead
to many relevant passages. Also, each key word may
have several English synonyms which will in turn lead
to more passages. For example, if you are studying the
topic of Christian finances, you might use quite a long
list of key words and synonyms, such as

   —*money, treasure, possessions*
   —*providence, provision, provide, supply*
   —*own, rich, poor*
   —*needs, necessity*
   —*stewardship*
   —*giving, tithe, tenth, offering*
   —*owe, debt, credit*
   —*taxes*
   —*greed*

When the word *gospel* is looked up in the concordance, it is discovered that our English word *gospel* is nearly always a translation of either *euaggelion* (literally meaning good news or good message) or *euaggelizomai* (literally meaning to tell or announce good news). This noun and verb are from the same Greek root. The index-lexicon or dictionary at the back of the concordance indicates that the word *euaggelion* is translated only into *gospel* in the King James Version. However, *euaggelizomai*, besides being translated into some phrases which use *gospel*, is also translated into some phrases which do not use *gospel*. Thus, these latter occurrences will not appear in the main body of the concordance under the word *gospel*. They must be found by looking up some of the other words in those phrases, such as *declare, preach, good tidings,* and *glad tidings.* The student must be careful to note which occurrences of these new words are derived from *euaggelizomai* rather than from other Greek words.

The use of these five English words *(gospel, declare, preach, good tidings,* and *glad tidings)* leads to all of the occurrences of this one Greek root—scores of passages. These passages must then be read in context, and the relevant passages must be tentatively sorted into the four categories described in chapter 18.

Four passages end up in category 1, Definitive-Long Passages: Acts 10:36-43; Acts 13:32-39; Romans 1:1-7; 1 Corinthians 15:1-8. (These are passages which *end up* in category 1 after further study in step 5.) Each of these passages meets all four of the requirements for category 1: definitely and directly on the subject; only one likely interpretation; not figurative; and extended.

More than a dozen passages end up in category 2, Definitive-Short Passages. Second Timothy 2:8 is typical of these passages. It meets all the requirements for category 1 except that it is brief rather than extended.

A few passages end up in category 3, Inferential Passages. Acts 15:1-11 is one of these passages. Verses 8-11 state the fact that both Jews and Gentiles are saved the same way—"by faith"; "through the grace of the Lord Jesus," rather than by being circumcised and keeping the law of Moses (compare vv. 1,5). The passage implies that the content of the gospel message which Peter preached to the Gentiles (v. 7) was in harmony with that fact. Thus, even though verse 7 does not explicitly state anything about the content of the gospel, the passage as a whole *implies* something about the content of the gospel and is thus placed in category 3.

A number of passages end up in category 4, Vague Passages. One of these passages is Romans 16:25, which states that according to Paul's gospel, God (compare v. 27) "is able to establish you." However, the precise meaning of this clause is not clear. A study of the word *establish (sterizo)* shows that it is used only a few times in the New Testament, and that it is a very general word which is used in a variety of senses. Thus, this verse is placed in category 4.

In most of the passages in category 4, the description of the gospel is limited to such phrases as "the gospel of the kingdom," "the gospel of God," or "the gospel of Christ." Such phrases do indicate that the content of the gospel message is generally related in some way to the kingdom, God, and Christ. However, these brief phrases do not give any specific information as to precisely what the gospel says about the kingdom, God, and Christ. *In themselves,* these passages would be open to varied interpretations, and thus they also are placed in category 4.

Step 5—Scrutinize

Beginning with the passages in category 1, each passage is scrutinized in turn. The four categories of passages are studied *in order* so that the less clear passages (categories 3 and 4) can be interpreted in the light of the clear passages (categories 1 and 2).

Only one passage is used as an illustration here, and only selected results from the use of the nine operations listed on page 191 are given. The passage is 1 Corinthians 15:1-8, one of the four passages in category 1.

a. Careful readings of 1 Corinthians 15:1-8 and its context, in different translations, reveal Paul's main point in this passage. He is restating the gospel message, namely, that Christ died for our sins, was buried, was raised on the third day, and then appeared alive to many people. The statement of this main point centers in the sentence in verses 3-5. The sentence in verses 1-2 tells about Paul's previous delivery of this message to the Corinthians. The sentence in verses 6-8 merely lists additional appearances of Christ to various individuals and groups.

First Corinthians 15:1-8 relates to the verses following it much more directly than it relates to the verses preceding it. In verses 12-58 Paul's argument regarding future resurrection is built upon the fact of Christ's past resurrection, which is an essential part of the gospel according to verses 4-8. In fact, Paul *may* have included the restatement of the gospel solely in order to lay a foundation for his long discussion of resurrection in the rest of the chapter. This *may* be the reason that Paul devotes more words to Christ's appearances (which verify his resurrection) than he devotes to any other aspect of the gospel.

b. I Corinthians 15:1-8 respaced

1   Now I make known to you, brethren,
          the gospel
               which I preached to you,
               which also you received,

in which also you stand,

2   by which also you are saved,

                    if you hold fast the word which I preached to you,

                    unless you believed in vain.

3   For I delivered to you as of first importance

            what I also received,

            that Christ died for our sins

                        according to the Scriptures,

4   and that He was buried,

            and that He was raised on the third day

                        according to the Scriptures,

5   and that He appeared

                    to Cephas,

                    then to the twelve.

6   After that He appeared to more than five hundred

                    brethren at one time,

                            most of whom remain until now,

                            but some have fallen asleep;

7   then He appeared to James,

            then to all the apostles;

8   as it were to one untimely born,

            and last of all,   He appeared to me also.

                                    (Author's underlines)

   c. I Corinthians 15:1-8 outlined:

Paul Restates the Gospel

  I. Paul's former delivery of the gospel and

      the Corinthians' response and benefit (1-3*a*)

 II. Paul's restatement of the content of that gospel (3*b*-8)

      A. Christ died and was buried (3*b*-4*a*)

      B. Christ was raised and appeared (4*b*-8)

   d. Many observations can be made by asking the questions who? when? where? what? how? and why? Only one such observation is mentioned here. Asking the question "when?" draws attention to, among other things, two references to time in verse 6. After his resurrection Jesus "appeared to more than five hundred brethren *at one time,* most of whom *remain until now,* but some have fallen asleep. . . ." If Paul merely wanted to list the postresurrection appearances of Jesus, it would seem that these time references are superfluous. Then how should they be interpreted? What is their significance? Consider the logical chain of ideas inherent in this passage. Paul's argument regarding future resurrection is supported by Christ's past resurrection, which in turn is supported by his postresurrection appearance to the more than five hundred brethren, which in turn is supported by two facts. First, they all saw Jesus "at one time" (which rules out hallucination in view of the extreme improbability of more than five hundred having the same hallucination simultaneously). Second, many of these brethren "remain until now" and could confirm that the appearance actually did take place. Because of these two facts the appearance to more than five hundred cannot be dismissed easily. This means that these two time references are very significant; they lend concrete support for Paul's teachings regarding resurrection.

e. A study of the grammatical details points up several interesting aspects of 1 Corinthians 15:1-8. For example, note the present tense in the clause in verse 2, "you are saved" (instead of "you were saved," or "you had been saved," or "you will be saved"). Also note the passive voice in the clauses in verses 2 and 4, "you are saved" (instead of "you save yourselves"), and "He was raised" (instead of "He raised Himself").

f. Many types of relationships can be identified in 1 Corinthians 15:1-8, such as the supportive relationship discussed in paragraph *d* above. Only one other will be mentioned here, namely, the evaluative relationship stated in verse 3. Paul says that four facts, about Christ's death, burial, resurrection, and appearances, were delivered to the Corinthians "as of first importance." This phrase indicates that, compared to any other facts which Paul could have told them, he evaluated these four as the most important. (Even though it is possible to translate this phrase differently, most translations use wording which means the same thing as the wording from the *New American Standard Bible* as quoted above.)

g. Many interesting temporary alterations in the wording of 1 Corinthians 15:1-8 can be made. Some of the most significant alterations have to do with the clause "Christ died for our sins" in verse 3. A few possible alterations are:

(1) Christ died for *his own* sins.

(2) Christ *showed us how we should die for our own sins.*

(3) Christ *suffered* for our sins *and appeared to die.*

(4) Christ died *because of the Jews' jealousy.*

(5) Christ died *because he was a threat to the Roman establishment.*

(6) Christ died for our *mistakes.*

(7) Christ died *as our example.*

(8) Christ died *as a martyr.*

(9) Christ died *with* our sins (our sins died with Christ).

(10) Christ died (omitting "for our sins" altogether).

By comparing such alterations with the "original" wording, we can better appreciate its significance. The sinlessness of Christ, his actual death, and his substitutionary payment of the penalty we owe for our own real sins, are all implied in this very weighty clause, "Christ died for our sins."

h. 1 Corinthians 15:1-8 paraphrased:

[1]Fellow Christians, I now repeat the same good news that I proclaimed to you before. You received it and still show confidence in it; [2]and you are saved by that same good news if you continue to adhere to it, unless you mistakenly trusted in something that cannot really save you. [3]For the message which I had received I then passed on to you—the most important truths—that Christ died because of our sins (in keeping with the Scriptures) [4]and was buried. Then on the third day he was brought back to life (in keeping with the Scriptures) [5]and personally presented himself to Cephas and to the twelve. [6]Furthermore, he later presented himself to a crowd of over five hundred followers (most of whom are still living) [7]as well as to James and to all the apostles. [8]Finally, he even presented himself to me, suddenly removing me from my former way of life.

i. 1 Corinthians 15:1-8 condensed:

> I declare to you the gospel which you have already received: Christ died for our sins, was buried, was raised, and then appeared to various individuals and groups, including me.

Step 6—Synthesize

The findings from all the definitive passages (the passages in categories 1 and 2) are now brought together to form conclusions and to answer the two basic questions.

The answer to the first basic question was given earlier: the word *gospel* means "good news."

Answering the second basic question requires much more thought and integration. This particular study,

Elements in the Gospel Message
from Definitive Passages Explicitly Linking these Elements with the Word Gospel

The Elements	Definitive- Long Passages			1 Corinthians 15:1-8	Selected Definitive- Short Passages
	Acts 10:36-43	Acts 13:32-39	Romans 1:1-7		
1. Sin	"Sins"	"Sins"	—	"Our sins"	—
2. Person of Jesus	"Jesus of Nazareth" "Jesus Christ (He is Lord of all)"	"Thou art my Son" "Thy Holy One"	"a descendant of David . . ." "The Son of God" "Jesus Christ our Lord"	—	"Descendant of David (2 Tim. 2:8)" "Jesus as the Christ" (Acts 5:42)
3. Death of Jesus	"Put Him to death by hanging Him on a cross"	"From the dead"	"From the dead"	"Died for our sins" "Buried"	"The cross of Christ" (1 Cor. 1:17-18) "The suffering of Christ" (1 Pet. 1:11)
4. Resurrection of Jesus	"God raised Him up on the third day" "Visible to witnesses who were chosen"	"He raised up Jesus" "No . . . . decay"	"The resurrection"	"He was raised on the third day" "He appeared to . . . "	"Preaching Jesus and the resurrection" (Acts 17:18) "Risen from the dead" (2 Tim. 2:8)

Other Aspects of the Gospel:

	"The gospel of peace through Jesus Christ" (margin)	"The good news of the promise ... that God has fulfilled ..."	"The gospel of God ... concerning His Son"	—	—
General statements				—	—
Response to the gospel	"Everyone who believes in Him ..."	"Everyone who believes ..."	"The obedience of faith"	"You believed"	"Repent and believe in the gospel" (Mark 1:15)
Result	"Received forgiveness of sins"	"Forgiveness of sins" "Freed from all things ..."	—	"By which ... you are saved"	"Hope laid up for you in heaven" (Col. 1:5)
The gospel is in keeping with O.T. Scripture	"Of Him all the prophets bear witness that ..."	"God has fulfilled this promise" "As it is ... written" etc.	"Promised beforehand through His prophets in the Holy Scriptures"	"According to the Scriptures"	—
Miscellaneous	"God anointed Him with the Holy Spirit and with power" "He went about doing good" "Healing all who were oppressed" "God was with Him" "Appointed ... Judge"	—	"Declared the Son of God by the resurrection"	"As of first importance"	"God will judge the secrets of men" (Rom. 2:16). "The glories to follow" (1 Pet. 1:10-12)

more than some others, lends itself to the use of a summary chart such as the one on pages 222-23. This chart includes the elements of the gospel which appear repeatedly in the definitive passages. The chart makes it quite obvious that there is a high degree of correlation among the definitive-long passages regarding what elements are included in the gospel message. And, of course, the definitive-short passages agree, even though they each include only one or two of the elements because of their brevity.

It is interesting to note that several of the other questions from step 2 are already at least partially answered by these definitive passages.

One simple way to summarize the content of the gospel message is to put all the relevant statements from all the definitive passages together into one long paragraph. The following paragraph is such a summary, following closely the wording of the *New American Standard Bible.*

> This is the gospel of God, which He promised beforehand through His prophets in the holy Scriptures. It is a message of first importance and concerns His Son—Jesus of Nazareth, Savior, Christ the Lord—who was born in the city of David and of the seed of David according to the flesh. God anointed Him with the Holy Spirit and with power. He went about doing good and healing all who were oppressed by the devil, for God was with Him. He preached, "The time is fulfilled, and the kingdom of God is at hand; repent and believe in the gospel." He suffered and died for our sins according to the Scriptures. The Jews put Him to death by hanging Him on a cross. Then He was buried.

Then God raised Him up from the dead on the third day according to the Scriptures, no more to undergo decay (unlike David and his fathers who underwent decay). This resurrection was promised to the fathers, and God has fulfilled this promise. Jesus was declared with power to be the Son of God by the resurrection from the dead, according to the Spirit of holiness. God granted that He should become visible, not to all the people, but to witnesses who were chosen beforehand by God, that is, to those who ate and drank with Him after He arose from the dead. He appeared to Cephas, then to the twelve. After that He appeared to more than five hundred brethren at one time, most of whom remain until now, but some have fallen asleep. Then He appeared to James, then to all the apostles; and last of all, as it were to one untimely born, He appeared to Paul also. Of Him all the prophets bear witness that through His name everyone, Jew or Gentile, who believes in Him (exercising the obedience of faith, holding fast the gospel) has received forgiveness of sins, and through Him everyone who believes is freed from all things, from which the Jews could not be freed through the Law of Moses. We are graciously saved by the gospel, receive peace through Him, and have a hope laid up for us in heaven. Jesus Christ is our Lord and the glorious Lord of all. He ordered us to preach to the people, and solemnly to testify that this is the One who has been appointed by God as Judge of the living and the dead, for God will judge the secrets of men through Christ Jesus.

A more difficult way to summarize the content of the gospel message is to attempt to state the *heart* or the *essential core* of the gospel in one sentence. In order to do this, it is necessary to examine the logical relationships (prerequisite, cause-effect, and supportive relationships) found either explicitly or implicitly in the definitive passages. The diagram on the next page attempts to represent some of these logical relationships.

As you carefully think through these relationships, it becomes apparent that Jesus' death for our sins and his resurrection form the logical core of the gospel. If we maintain that Jesus died for our sins and rose again, then logically we must also maintain that we have sinned (else how could he die for them?), that Jesus is divine (being declared the Son of God by the resurrection), and that Jesus lived a sinless life (as necessitated by his divine nature). In other words, maintaining the essential core of the gospel logically necessitates much of the rest of the chart. Furthermore, this logical necessity works only one way; it is not reciprocal. Jesus' death for our sins and his resurrection logically necessitate Jesus' divine person and his sinless life, but his divine person and sinless life do not *logically* necessitate his death for our sins and resurrection. For this reason the death and resurrection are considered to be the heart and essential core of the gospel.

Because of these logical relationships, the heart of the gospel can be stated in its simplest terms as follows:

Jesus Christ died for our sins and rose again.

If a person adequately appreciates the significance of this statement, the rest of the ideas on the chart should easily fall into place for him. It is very interesting to note that this statement of the heart of the gospel, which

Logical Relationships Inherent in the Definite Passages which State the Content of the Gospel Message

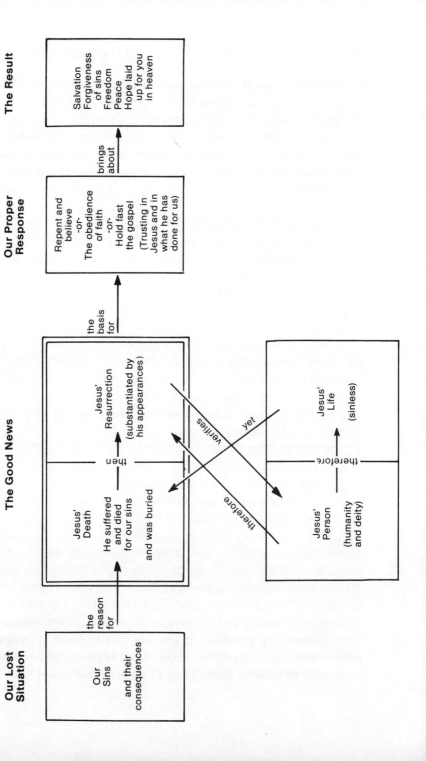

is derived from a consideration of the logical relationships, corresponds closely with what Paul labels "as of
first importance" in 1 Corinthians 15:3-5.

In answer to the second basic question, then, the following facts are listed as those which a person must
understand and consider true before he can respond to
the gospel.

    1. Our sins and their consequences
    2. Jesus' divine (as well as human) nature
    3. Jesus' sinless life
    4. Jesus' suffering and death for *our* sins
    5. Jesus' resurrection

Upon understanding these facts and considering them
true, a person can then respond by trusting in Jesus and
in what he has done for us. Or, of course, one can respond by rejecting Jesus. If one trusts, one receives
salvation, forgiveness, freedom, peace, and hope.

This study has isolated several key topics which deserve further study.

    —sin and its consequences
    —the person of Jesus
    —the death of Jesus (especially the substitu-
      tionary aspect of his death)
    —repentance, belief, and faith

Each of these topics deserves a thorough study of its
own. It should be kept in mind that this present study is
based only on those passages which use the Greek word
for *gospel* and which explicitly say something about the
content of the gospel message. However, after isolating
the various facts which make up the gospel, it is quite
apparent that the Bible says a great deal more about
each of these facts than what is included in the definitive

passages of this present study. For example, have you noticed how little the definitive passages say about God's attributes of holiness, justice, and love, or about the response of works as an improper means of gaining salvation? Yet these are definitely related to the gospel. Thus, follow-up studies would be very profitable in expanding your appreciation of this topic. And, of course, there are still many questions left over from step 2 which could also form the basis for further study.

Step 7—Compare

Step 8—Apply

The most obvious application growing out of this study is the response described in the definitive passages themselves. Since Jesus died for our sins and rose again, we ought to trust in him and in what he has done for us. For those who are already trusting in Jesus, another application is also important.

When we share the gospel with someone else, we must present the content of the gospel message accurately, being especially careful to include the heart of the gospel. Many so-called evangelistic messages, gospel tracts, and personal witnessing encounters do not adequately explain Jesus' death for our sins and his resurrection. If a person is not told the heart of the gospel, in what does he place his trust? When we share the gospel, we must be sure that it *is* the gospel.

Appendix C
Sample Respaced Texts

These three brief samples are respaced according to the following rules:

1. No changes are made in the wording or punctuation of the text.

2. Connectives and conjunctions are studied carefully since they often signal the start of a new thought unit.

3. Main statements begin at the left margin.

4. Other statements are indented appropriately.

5. Modifying phrases and clauses often begin under the word they modify.

6. Sometimes modifying phrases located within a clause are respaced above the clause to reveal the uninterrupted flow of thought in that clause.

7. Consecutive parallel thought units begin directly under each other.

8. A broken line is sometimes used to indicate antecedent relationships.

9. Key words and clauses are underlined.

Genesis 1:1-5[1]

1   In the beginning
      <u>God created the heavens</u>
            <u>and the earth.</u>

2   And the earth was <u>formless and void,</u>

and darkness was over the surface of the deep;
and the Spirit of God was moving over the surface of
the waters.

3   Then God said, "Let there be light";
and there was light.

4   And God saw that the light was good;
and God separated the light from the darkness.

5   And God called the light day,
and the darkness He called night.

And there was evening
and there was morning,
one day.

Psalm 1

1   How blessed is the man
who does not walk in the counsel of the wicked,
Nor stand in the path of sinners,
Nor sit in the seat of scoffers!

2   But in his delight is in the law of the Lord,
And in His law he meditates
day and night.

3   And he will be like a tree
firmly planted by streams of water,
Which yields its fruit in its season,
And its leaf does not wither;
And in whatever he does, he prospers.

4   The wicked are not so,
But they are like chaff
which the wind drives away.

5   Therefore the wicked will not stand in the judgment,
Nor sinners in the assembly of the righteous,

6   For the Lord knows the way of the righteous,
But the way of the wicked will perish.

James 3:13-18

13   among you

Who   is wise and understanding?

          by his good behavior

Let him show   his deeds

       in the gentleness of wisdom.

14   But if you have bitter jealousy and selfish ambition

        in your heart,

     do not be arrogant

       and so lie against the truth.

15   This wisdom is not that which comes down from above,

       but is earthly,

          natural,

          demonic.

16   For where jealously and selfish ambition exist,

         there is disorder and every evil thing.

17   But the wisdom from above is first pure,

           then peaceable,

            gentle,

            reasonable,

            full of mercy and good fruits,

            unwavering,

            without hypocrisy.

18   whose fruit is righteous

    And the seed   is sown in peace

          by those who make peace.

Note

1. Author's underlines in all three passages.

Appendix D
Diagrams and Examples of Types of Relationships

Diagrams

The diagrams in this appendix are intended to picture some of the types of relationships described in chapter 17. You should compare these diagrams with those descriptions. Caution: A diagram, like a parable, can effectively show only one truth (one type of relationship) at a time. Furthermore, often the same diagram will mean different things to different people.

If you tend to think pictorially or graphically, you may want to make your own diagrams of the key relationships you find in a biblical text, and the following samples may help you create your own.

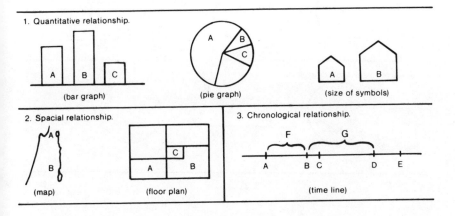

1. Quantitative relationship.

(bar graph)   (pie graph)   (size of symbols)

2. Spacial relationship.

(map)   (floor plan)

3. Chronological relationship.

(time line)

4. Sequential relationship.

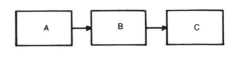

5. Cyclical relationship.

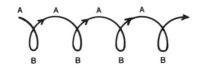

6. Reciprocating or vice versa relationship.

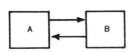
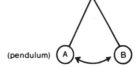

7. Cause-effect or parent-offspring relationship.

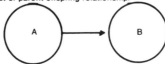

8. Agency or means-end relationship.

Starting point   Means   End

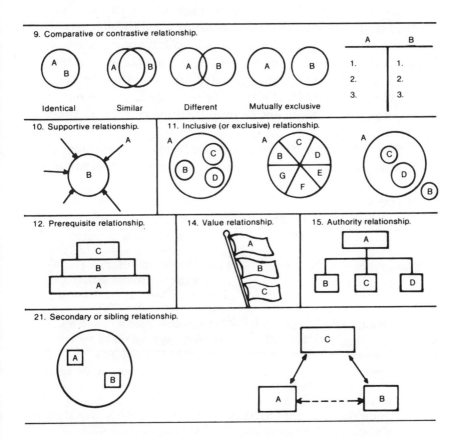

9. Comparative or contrastive relationship.

Identical   Similar   Different   Mutually exclusive

10. Supportive relationship.

11. Inclusive (or exclusive) relationship.

12. Prerequisite relationship.

14. Value relationship.

15. Authority relationship.

21. Secondary or sibling relationship.

Examples

The following examples, taken mostly from 1 Corinthians, illustrate all of the types of relationships described in chapter 17. In order for these examples to be most helpful, they should be compared with those descriptions, and each passage should be read before the explanation is read.

Even though the following examples point out only one type of relationship for each reference, you may often find that two items in the text are related to each other in more than one way. For example, both a quantitative and a value relationship are found in 1 Corinthians 14:19.

In some of the examples below, the relationship is explicitly stated in the text. When this is the case, that explicit word or phrase is usually quoted in parentheses with the explanation.

Some of the relationships in the following examples are stated literally in the text; some are stated figuratively.

Type of Relationship	Reference	Explanation
1. Quantitative	1 Cor. 14:19	Ten thousand words are much much *greater in number* than five words. (Of course, the fact that Paul prefers the five words indicates that they are greater in instructional value.)
1. Quantitative	Num. 13:32-33	The Israelites were so much *shorter* than the Nephilim that they saw themselves as grasshoppers.

2. Spacial—The most common means of noting large-scale spacial relationships is with the aid of maps. However, occasionally spacial relationships on a smaller scale are also important to observe, such as the floor plan and furnishings of the tabernacle (Ex. 25—27), and the seating of the disciples at the Last Supper (John 13:21-25).

3. Chronological—The historical books of the Bible supply numerous events which can be related to each other chronologically, perhaps even placed on a time line. However, even more didactic books often contain events that can be arranged chronologically, such as the fifteen or more distinct events mentioned in 1 Corinthians 15:1-9.

    —Christ died for our sins.

    —Christ was buried.

      —Christ was raised on the third day.

        —Christ appeared to Cephas.

        —Christ appeared to the twelve.

—Christ appeared to more than five hundred brethren.
—Christ appeared to James.
—Christ appeared to all the apostles.
—Paul persecuted the church.
—Christ appeared to Paul.
—Paul received the gospel.
—Paul preached the gospel to the Corinthians.
—The Corinthians received the gospel.
—The Corinthians hold it fast and are saved.
—Paul makes the gospel known (again) to the Corinthians.

4. Sequential	Prov. 16:18	Pride and a haughty spirit go *"before"* destruction and stumbling.
5. Cyclical	1 Cor. 11:1	Christ's example is imitated by Paul; *in turn*, Paul's example is to be imitated by the Corinthians.
5. Cyclical	2 Tim. 2:2	Paul taught Timothy, who *in turn* taught faithful men, who *in turn* taught others.
6. Reciprocating or vice versa	1 Cor. 7:3-4	The husband's duty to his wife is the *same* as ("likewise") the wife's duty to her husband. The husband has authority over the wife's body, and *vice versa* ("likewise").
6. Reciprocating or vice versa	Rom. 1:11-12	Paul hoped to *encourage* the Romans and to *be encouraged by* the Romans ("each of us by the other's faith").
7. Cause-effect or parent-offspring	1 Cor. 11:29-30	Eating and drinking without rightly judging the body *causes* ("for this reason") sickness and death among the Corinthians.
8. Agency or means-end	1 Cor. 9:19-22	Becoming as a Jew, as without the law, etc. are the various *means* or methods ("by all means") used by Paul in order to win more.

9. Comparative or contrastive	1 Cor. 9:13-14	The idea that those who preach the gospel should be paid is *similar* to the idea that those who perform sacred services eat the food of the Temple, etc. ("so also").
9. Comparative or contrastive	1 Cor. 1:25	God's wisdom and strength are *contrasted* with man's ("wiser than," "stronger than").
9. Comparative or contrastive	1 Cor. 10:21	Fellowship with the Lord and fellowship with demons are *mutually exclusive* practices ("you cannot . . . and").
9. Comparative or contrastive	2 Cor. 11:13-15	The false apostles' pattern of operation (disguising themselves) is *identical* to Satan's pattern of operation ("no wonder," "even," "it is not surprising, "also").
9. Comparative or contrastive	Matt. 20:25-28	Greatness among the disciples is simultaneously *contrasted* with the supposed greatness of the Gentile rulers and *compared* with the greatness of Jesus ("it is not so among you," "just as").

Comparisons and contrasts abound in the Bible, sometimes even occupying extended portions, such as the contrasts between law and grace in Galatians and between the old and new covenants in Hebrews. The side-by-side column analysis mentioned in chapter 17 is especially helpful in connection with these more extended and more complex comparisons and contrasts.

10. Supportive	1 Cor. 2:7-8	The fact that the rulers crucified the Lord is *evidence* that supports the proposition that they did not understand God's wisdom ("for").
10. Supportive	1 Cor. 7:2	Abundant immorality is the *reason* why a man should have a wife and a

		woman should have a husband ("because of").
11. Inclusive (or exclusive)	1 Cor. 1:1 and 15:7-8	In chapter 1, Paul *includes* himself among the apostles. In chapter 15, Paul *excludes* himself from among the apostles.
12. Prerequisite	1 Cor. 13:1-3	Love is *necessary* for the gifts of tongues, prophecy, etc. to be worthwhile and significant.
12. Prerequisite	Rom. 10:14-15	Sending *must take place before* preaching can take place, preaching before hearing, etc.
13. Inferential	1 Cor. 3:14	*If* a man's work remains, *then* he shall receive a reward.
13. Inferential	1 Cor. 7:39	*If* her husband is dead, *then* she is free to remarry.
14. Value	1 Cor. 7:19	Whether or not one keeps God's commandments is vastly *more important than* whether or not one is circumcised.
14. Value	1 Cor. 14:5	The one who prophesies is of *more value than* the one who speaks in uninterpreted tongues ("greater").
14. Value	1 Cor. 14:19	Paul's desire to speak a few instructive words rather than many unintelligible words implies that prophecy is *more valuable than* tongue-speaking.
15. Authority	1 Cor. 11:3-5,10	The husband has authority over the wife ("head," "authority").
16. Attributional	1 Cor. 4:2	Trustworthiness is one of the *qualities* required of stewards.

16. Attributional	1 Cor. 4:20	Power is one of the *characteristics* of the kingdom of God; mere talk is not ("consist").
17. Illustrative	1 Cor. 4:1-6	Paul *applies* the concept of humility to himself and Apollos in order to serve as an *example* to the arrogant Corinthians ("I have . . . applied . . .that in us you might learn").
17. Illustrative	1 Cor. 14:7-9	The meaninglessness of unintelligible words is *illustrated* by the meaninglessness of unintelligible sounds coming from a flute, harp, or bugle ("so also you").
17. Illustrative	Phil. 2:3-8	What Jesus did is an *example* of the humble, servant attitude commanded in verses 3-4 ("which was also in Christ Jesus").
18. Evaluative	1 Cor. 7:1,8	Remaining single is *evaluated* by the phrase "it is good."
18. Evaluative	1 Cor. 15:3	The information that Paul delivered to the Corinthians is *evaluated* by the phrase "of first importance."
19. Problem-solution or question-answer	1 Cor. 14:1-40	Paul's instructions about orderliness and the proper use of tongues implies that this chapter is the *solution* to the Corinthian *problem* of the disruption of their meetings through the misuse of tongues.
20. Principle-application	1 Cor. 4:17	Paul *applies* his own teachings in his own life ("my ways . . . just as I teach").
20. Principle-application	Phil. 4:9	The principles which the Philippians have learned are to be

		put into practice ("practice these things").
21. Secondary or sibling	1 Cor. 12:14-16	Even though the foot, hand, ear, and eye are diverse, they hold equal status with each other *because* they are all *parts of* one body.
21. Secondary or sibling	Gal. 3:26-29	The Galatians had a *secondary relationship* to each other (oneness, fellow heirs) because of their *primary relationship* to Christ ("in Christ," "belonging to Christ").
22. Unrelated	1 Cor. 8:8	One's relationship to God is *completely independent* of eating, or not eating, food offered to an idol.

Appendix E

A Note to Pastors and Teachers

If you plan to use this guidebook in a course on personal Bible study, remember that DBD must be experienced in order to be really appreciated, and it must be practiced in order to become a usable skill. Thus, any course in personal Bible study should be taught with a minimum of lecture and a maximum of student practice. Here are some suggestions for using this guidebook in a course in your local church, college, or seminary.

1. It is important for the students to gain an overview of the entire DBD approach before they try to apply it in actual Bible study. Thus, the students should be asked to read this entire guidebook at the very beginning of the course. Unless the students grasp DBD as a unified and reasoned way of studying the Bible, their use of the procedures could be quite mechanical and meaningless. As pastor or teacher, you should evaluate your students' comprehension of the basic DBD approach, principles, and procedures. Feedback from your students (such as discussions, a series of quizzes, etc., or a combination of these) will allow you to diagnose weaknesses in their understanding of DBD. You can then deal specifically with whatever misunderstandings you uncover. This can forestall problems which would arise later when the students attempt to put the principles and procedures to use in the actual study of the Bible.

2. During the first several sessions, while the students are reading this guidebook outside of class, you should supplement this material with your own ideas. Also, during these first several sessions, you should give the students exercise (on short, isolated Bible passages) in the most basic skill of DBD, namely, systematic observation.

3. After the students understand the basic principles and procedures, and after they have had experience in systematic observation, the greater part of the course should be devoted to the actual use of DBD procedures on at least one short Bible book and at least one simple Bible topic. Avoid the temptation to teach the book or the topic. Instead, teach your students to use the principles and procedures so that they teach themselves the book or the topic. Your goal should be to teach them to *discover* on their own and to *think* on their own so that they will be able to carry out meaningful personal Bible study without your help in the future. Through the careful use of questions, stimulate and guide your students.

4. Introduce the skills *gradually.* For example, after the students have surveyed and divided a book, do not assign all twelve operations in step 4 at one time. Instead, allow the students to focus on two or three of the skills in each assignment. This is most critical when the students are first learning to carry out these operations. Students can easily become discouraged unless they feel the sense of satisfaction which comes with some degree of mastery of each skill. After the students have gained confidence in their ability to perform each operation, then more, or perhaps all, of step 4 can be assigned at once.

Annotated Bibliography[1]

Personal Bible Study

Adler, Mortimer J. and Charles Van Doren. *How to Read a Book*, New York: Simon and Schuster, 1972.

Although this book is not specifically about reading the Bible, it explains many principles which are very helpful when applied to Bible study.

Jensen, Irving L. *Independent Bible Study—Using the Analytical Chart and the Inductive Method.* Chicago: Moody Press, 1963.

Stresses the inductive analysis of Bible passages and the visual representation (charting) of their grammatical and literary structure. Reflects much of Traina.

Kinsler, F. Ross. *Inductive Study of the Book of Mark.* South Pasadena, California: William Carey Library, 1972.

An inductive study which includes thorough explanations of the various direct study procedures employed so that the approach learned here is easily transferred to other books of the Bible. A programmed text. Kinsler has also written two similar volumes: *Inductive Study of the Book of Romans* and *Inductive Study of the Book of Jeremiah.*

Perry, Lloyd M. and Robert D. Culver. *How to Search the Scriptures.* Grand Rapids, Michigan: Baker, 1967.

Covers basic facts about the Scriptures, many testi-
monials regarding Bible study procedures, and
brief explanations with extensive examples of various "methods" of personal Bible study.

Richards, Lawrence O. *Creative Bible Study.* Grand
Rapids, Michigan: Zondervan, 1971.

Discusses fundamental principles of individual and
group Bible study stressing the thoughtful study
and life-application of the Bible.

Sterrett, T. Norton, *How to Understand Your Bible,* rev.
ed. Downers Grove, Illinois: Inter-Varsity Press, 1974.

Contains excellent explanations and illustrations of
many important principles regarding both hermeneutics and Bible study.

Tenney, Merrill C. *Galatians: The Charter of Christian
Liberty.* Grand Rapids, Michigan: William B. Eerdmans, 1950.

A classic example of the study of a Bible book from
many different angles. Each chapter explains and
then applies a different method. (That is, each
chapter looks at a different aspect of the book of
Galatians.) The nine aspects examined are the
synthetic (overview), critical (background), biographical, historical, theological, rhetorical, topical,
analytical, and devotional aspects. Each chapter
adds significantly both to one's understanding of
the book of Galatians and to one's appreciation of the
value of that particular "method" of Bible study.

Traina, Robert A. *Methodical Bible Study—A New Approach to Hermeneutics.* Robert A. Traina, 1952.

A classic statement of inductive Bible study. It focuses on the analysis of small units of Scripture. The
chapter on observation contains a long and technical
discussion on investigating the structure of a Bible
passage. The chapter on interpretation discusses in-

terpretive questions and answers, many hermeneutical principles, and exposes many faulty types of
interpretation. The book is very detailed and analytical, and its terminology is difficult for the average
reader, but the careful reading of this work is well
worth the effort. (Available directly from Dr. Robert
A. Traina, 505 Bellevue Ave., Wilmore, KY 40390.)

Wald, Oletta. *The Joy of Discovery in Bible Study,* rev. ed.
Minneapolis, Minnesota: Augsburg Publishing House,
1975.

Many excellent suggestions regarding the skills
and practices used in inductive Bible study, including examples and exercises. Even though Wald
refers to this book as a "workbook" based on Traina,
it can easily and profitably be used by itself. A companion volume by Wald, *The Joy of Teaching Discovery Bible Study,* is also available from Augsburg.

Note

1. Resources for hermeneutics are given on pp. 94-95,
and a discussion of various interpretive aids is found on
pp. 150-151.

Index

Agassiz, 77-81
Aids: interpretive, 37-43, 150-151; noninterpretive, 43, 148-150
Allegorical interpretation, 105-106
Allegory, 100
Altering the wording, 177
Analogy, argument by, 124-125
Analysis, (see Scrutiny)
Anthropomorphism, 100-101, 104
Apostrophe, 100
Application: in relation to observation and interpretation, 56-58, 83; multiple applications, 91; making application, 131-136; examples and commands not necessarily binding, 132-135; the "devotional method," 135-136; as part of book study, 182
Assumptions, 29-32, 34-35, 45-52, 59-61, 63-65, 71-72, 121-122, 139
Atlas, 150
Attitude, 17-18, 85

Background of a book, 163-165
Bereans, 42-44, 53
Bird's-eye view, 137-138
Book study: in relation to topic study, 138-139; recommendations for first few book studies, 139-142; procedure, chapter 17
Books for use in Bible study, 148-151

Canon, 55-56
Categories of passages in topic study, 189-190
Charting a book, 166-168, 206
Christian living: active or passive, 22-24; partial list of areas, 144-146
Circular reasoning, 49, 121
Commentaries, (see Aids, interpretive)
Comparing passage with passage, 116-119

Comparing your interpretation with others', 40, 182, 195
Concordance, 150, 187-189
Condensing, 180
Context, chapter 12; immediate context and larger context, 109; "Immediate Context Unit," 166
Contradictions, 117-119
Converse, 126-127

Deduction, 46-48, 106
Definition of "Direct Bible Discovery," 14
Definition versus partial description, 128-129
Definitive-long passages, 189
Definitive-short passages, 190
Delimiting a topic, 186
Devotional method, 135-136
Devotions, 156
Dictionary, English, 149-150
"Direct Bible Discovery" defined, 14
Direct procedure, chapter 4
Discovery procedure, chapter 5
Dispensations, 111-112
Dividing a book, 165-167, 203-204
Doctrinal study, (see Topics)

Eisegesis, 49
Etymology, 115, 192-193
Euphemism, 101, 105
Evangelism, Appendix B
Exclamatory rhetorical question, 102
Exegesis, chapter 5 and page 56, 83
Extending assumptions, 46-52

Figurative interpretation, (see Literary interpretation)
Figures of speech, 99-106
Finding and sorting passages on a topic, 186-190
First-mention principle, 117
Fish, The, 77-81

Gospel, Appendix B
Grammatical details, 175
Greek and Hebrew: preference for, 88; study helps, 89; caution regarding overdependence on Greek and Hebrew, 89-90
Group study, 156-157

Hebrew, (see Greek and Hebrew)
Hermeneutics, 56-57 and chapters 10, 11, 12
Holy Spirit: how he teaches, chapter 2; inspiration and preservation of the Bible, 55-56; guidance, illumination, empowering, 56-57
Hyperbole, 101
Hypothetical conjecture, 102-103

ICU, 166
Idioms, 114-115
"Immediate Context Unit," 166
Indirect procedure, 37-38
Induction, 45-48, 176
Inferential passages, 190
Inspiration, 55-56, 85
Interpretation: comparing your interpretation with others', 40, 182, 195; in relation to observation and application, 56-58; distinguished from observation, chapter 7 and page 73; sample interpretations on "Mary Had a Little Lamb," 62-65; sample interpretations on Mark 2:1-12, 71-73; of the Bible different from interpretation of nonbiblical literature, 84-86; principles or rules of interpretation, chapters 10, 11, 12; the interpreter's task, 86-88; preference for the original languages, 88-90; singularity of interpretation, 90-91; recording interpretations, 91-92; literary interpretation, chapter 11; context, chapter 12; historical and cultural interpretation, 113-115; comparing passage with passage, 116-119
Interrogation, 102
Inverse, 126-127

Irony, 103

Literal interpretation, chapter 11
Literary interpretation, chapter 11
Literature, types of in the Bible, 140-141, 163
Litotes, 99
Logic, (see Reasoning)

Maps, 150
Marking in your Bible, 149
"Mary Had a Little Lamb," 62-65
Meditation, 14-16
Memorization, 157-158
Metaphor, 100, 104
Methods, 16, 138
Metonymy, 101
Motivation, 17-18, 132

Notebook, 148-149

Objectivity, 75-76, 185, 190
Observation: in relation to interpretation and
   application, 56-58; distinguished from interpretation,
   chapter 7 and page 73; sample observations on "Mary
   Had a Little Lamb," 62-65; suggestions regarding
   making observations, 67-69, 73, 167-181; sample
   observations on Mark 2:1-12, 70-71; pitfalls in making
   observations, 75-77; done the same way for biblical
   and nonbiblical literature, 84; recording observations,
   91; observation-interpretation-application form, 170
Open-mindedness, 52-53, 75-76
Outlining, 160, 173-174
Overgeneralization, 122
Overview, (see Surveying)

Parable, 99-100
Parallel passages, 116-117
Paraphrased versions, 152-153

Paraphrasing, 177-180
Patience, 92-93
Perseverance in Bible study, 77-81
Personification, 100
Philippians, Appendix A
Place for Bible study, 148
Presuppositions, (see Assumptions)
Principles of interpretation, (see Hermeneutics, and
    Interpretation)
Procedure: importance of procedure, chapter 3; facts
    about procedure, 27-32; facts about procedure applied
    to Bible study, 32-35; everyone has a procedure, 33;
    direct procedure, chapter 4; discovery procedure,
    chapter 5; procedure versus meaning, 159-160;
    procedure for studying books, chapter 17; procedure
    for studying topics, chapter 18
Progressive revelation, 111-112
Prooftext, 34, 49

Questions, 92-93, 173-174
Quiet time, 156

Reading for meaning, 160, 169
Reasoning, chapter 13: circular reasoning, 121-122;
    overgeneralization, 122; argument from silence,
    122-124; argument by analogy, 124-125; improper
    inference, 125-127; definition versus partial
    description, 128
Recalling present ideas on a topic, 186
Relationships, 175-176, 178-179: diagrams and
    examples, Appendix D
Respacing: explained, 171-173, 231; samples, 69-70,
    204-205, 217-218, and Appendix C
Rhetorical question, 102
Rules of interpretation, (see Hermeneutics, and
    Interpretation)

Scrutiny: scrutinizing an ICU, 167-181; scrutinizing

passages in a topic study, 190-191
Secondary issues, 93-94
Silence, argument from, 122-124
Simile, 99
Small groups, 156-157
Sorting passages in a topic study, 189-190
"Spiritualizing" the text, 105-106
Steps, (see Procedure)
Student, The, 77-81
Subjectivity, 75-76
Subjects, (see Topics)
Summarizing, 180, 181-182
Summary of principles, chapter 19
Sunday School classes, 156-157
Surveying: the whole Bible, 137-138; a book, 162-165
Symbol, 101-102
Synecdoche, 101
Synthesizing, 181-182, 195

Textual criticism, 55-56, 154
Textus Receptus, 154
Time for Bible study, 147-148
Tools, (see Aids)
Topics: topic study in relation to book study, 138-139;
    list of doctrinal topics, 142-144; list of areas of
    Christian living, 144-146; suggestions for first few
    topic studies, 146; within a book, 181; procedure,
    chapter 18
Translation: idiomatic, 114-115; choosing a translation,
    151-156; accuracy, 152-153; paraphrases, 152-153;
    use of current English, 153-154; committee
    translation, 154-155; annotations to the translation,
    155; recommended translations, 155

Vague passages, 108, 117-118, 190, 194-195
Versions of the Bible, (see Translations)

Whole-parts-whole, 161-162
Word studies, 115, 191-194, 213-216